FREEDOM
AND THE COLLEGE

FREEDOM
AND THE COLLEGE

BY
ALEXANDER MEIKLEJOHN

Essay Index Reprint Series

BOOKS FOR LIBRARIES PRESS
FREEPORT, NEW YORK

INTERNATIONAL STANDARD BOOK NUMBER:
0-8369-1990-4

LIBRARY OF CONGRESS CATALOG CARD NUMBER:
75-99641

PRINTED IN THE UNITED STATES OF AMERICA

TO THEM THAT
"GOON ON PILGRIMAGES"

CONTENTS

INTRODUCTION

THESE papers are attempts to define and to describe the teaching and the learning of Freedom. In all of them the underlying question is, How can a people be kept steadfast in its determination to be free; how can citizens, young or old, be trained to be intelligent and efficient in the pursuit of freedom of activity?

With one exception, these papers were all written during the last six years, that is, since the entering of the United States into the Great War. I am interested to note, as I read them again, that, with one exception, these later papers are all affected by what we call the "post-war state of mind." It may be worth while to make allowance for this fact as the papers are read. May I therefore state it a little more fully?

The first paper, of which exception has just been made, is an address given at my inauguration as president of Amherst College in 1912; the second was read at the centennial celebration of the college in 1921. When the first was given war was not expected nor was it even thought pos-

sible by most of us.   And again when the college
held its days of celebration we seemed for the moment to escape from the dismay and depression
which had come upon us as we tasted the fruits
of victory.   My own theme on that occasion was,
What does the college hope to be during the next
hundred years?   Under the stimulus of that theme
it was easy to make even the Great War seem only
a step, an incident, in the march of men toward
freedom.

But between these two papers and the others
there will be found, I think, a sharp, disturbing
contrast.   In all this later group negation is
strong.   The purpose is the same but now the
purpose seems to tarry.   The Inaugural had
asked, What must a college give?   And it had
answered plain and flat and confident, It must
give Insight.   At the Centennial we asked, What
will the college be in coming years?   And here
again the answer was in terms of hope and res-
olution.   We talked of this young country and its
colleges; we found in them Democracy, Idealism, and Faith.   But in the other group of
papers the reader will hear another note.   In
every one of them there is complaint, there is a
"but" that speaks dismay.   Are we a Christian
people?   Yes, but we do not act as Christians

say that Christians should. We play at games
in colleges. But do we really play; have we not
made of games a something else which robs them
of their meaning? We make machines to help
us in our work. Are they not using us; are they
not making us their instruments for ends which
no one has conceived? If Insight is to come
from college teaching, this teaching must have
unity and meaning in itself. But in our college
teaching as we have it now there is no unity or
meaning. The college course must be reor-
ganized, be made to suit its present urgent purpose. Where shall we find a college that has
enough of freedom in its spirit to do the things
that must be done?

These "buts" and queries, I say again, are
incidents in thinking and living after a war. The
task of taking one's spirit over from war to
peace is not an easy one. And colleges, as
well as individuals and other social groups, must
take their share of bitterness and strife and dis-
illusion. My own impression is that we are suffering less than might have been expected. We
suffer too much, I know. There is too much
intolerance, too much suppression of freedom in
action, thought, and speech, too much vindictive
persecution of those who tried to save our souls

while war was on, too much of selfish gloating over spoils which in the course of war we won from friend as well as foe. And, worst of all, we have too much the vice on which war feeds, the sense of moral rightness in ourselves, in terms of which we visit condemnation on our fellow-men, here or abroad. This is the vice by means of which, when interests clash, we make the other man, by sheer imagination, into something vile and wrong; then we can fight him with good conscience, can take the side of God, our God, against the devil. Of all these things we have too much. And yet, I say, we have them less than might have been expected. For us the war is going past. It did not really get us in its grip. Soon, I believe, we shall be on the road again. In spite of persecutions here and there, in spite of much timidity and "playing safe," the general spirit is not daunted. It soon will find its way. And as it goes its way, so will the colleges. They are, I think, upon the threshold of a venture such as colleges have never seen. Their day is coming as it never came before.

Thus far I have not spoken of the third period of the book. It too was written in the period to which the others belong. But in its origins and sentiments it goes back to my own undergraduate

days and to the man whom, with hundreds of my
fellows, I then took as hero. The paper is a
study of Elisha Benjamin Andrews who became
president of Brown University in the fall of 1889,
when I was entering college as a freshman. It
was read at Brown as a tribute to Andrews, in
May, 1918, a few months after he died.

I need not in this introduction tell again the
qualities of Andrews which made men love and
follow him. I should like, however, to speak of
one aspect of him which later experience has
brought to me with peculiar vividness. More
than any other man whom I have known in college office, Andrews mastered administration,
made it his servant, kept it in its proper place.
He hated busyness as healthy men hate shopping.
I sometimes think no man should be allowed to
have administration in his charge unless he
loathes it, unless he wishes to be doing something
else. I dare not trust the willing middlemen of
life, the men who like arranging other men and
their affairs, who find manipulation satisfying to
their souls. These men if they can have their
way will make of life a smooth, well lubricated
meaninglessness. Andrews was not like that.
He was a scholar and teacher. He knew that
colleges exist for teaching and study, and what he

cared for was that study and teaching should be done. He was a maker of men because he had a mad, impetuous vision of what a man may be. He wanted something done, something accomplished in the spirit of man. For him administration was Idea guiding and controlling circumstance. It was not, as many men demand it should be made, mere circumstances slipping smoothly past each other in the flow of time.

More than any one else whom I have known in academic life, Andrews gave to me the dream of having freedom, of being free and yet in action. As I look back now over twenty-two years of college administration, eleven as dean, eleven as president, I welcome this opportunity to pay tribute to him who boldly tried to make administration do its proper work, who kept it in its proper place.

ALEXANDER MEIKLEJOHN.

TO WHOM ARE WE RESPONSIBLE?

A MEMORANDUM ON THE FREEDOM OF TEACHERS
"THE CENTURY MAGAZINE," SEPTEMBER, 1923

FREEDOM AND THE COLLEGE

TO WHOM ARE WE RESPONSIBLE?

§ 1

THE question of this paper is, as we say, an elusive one. When such a question gets answered, it often happens that the question has disappeared. In the process of inquiry another question has taken the place of the one with which we started. If we would avoid such discomfiture, such substitution of mental changelings, it is essential that the mind hold fast to its own. We must grasp our question, define it, define its terms, and hold them fast, keep them defined, until the end is reached.

Who, then, are "we"? The question is here asked about the persons who are in charge of colleges. Who are they? Any one who knows what a college is knows that in this case "we" means faculty and president. These two have charge of study and teaching. Our question is about them.

May I stop to note what a pity it is that the Association of University Professors has defined the term "we" so badly? This association was founded to advance the interests of learning and teaching. It has summoned teachers to the work, but has excluded presidents from the fellowship. In so doing it has followed a drift which it ought rather to have opposed and overcome. Nearly every influence in a college tends to separate president from faculty, tends to make of him an administrator rather than a student, tends to give him connection with trustees and alumni and donors rather than with teachers. But he needs the teachers. His soul needs ever to be saved to that kingdom of learning of which he is in some sense in charge. Nevertheless, the teachers, by a timid, defensive manœuver, have consigned him to the company of publicans and sinners. They ought to see that, rightly or wrongly, the president of a college has power to affect research and teaching; that, rightly or not, he is responsible for research and teaching; that, whether they wish it or not, he is their fellow and shares with them their chief responsibility. But in general I should say that in recent years professors have done what they could to make presidents unfit for their responsibilities. On behalf of the much rejected and bedamned I demand that they be given a chance to save their souls. They and the faculties are, and must be, responsible for teaching and research. These two are the "we" in this discussion.

But, second, what do we mean by "responsible"? This is a shifty term which often slips and slides under the careless fingers of human thinking. My own present definition is worked out from watching a traffic policeman and from reading Epictetus. Each brings out one aspect of a double meaning. If we separate the two aspects, we may hold apart in some clearness "responsible for" and "responsible to." The policeman has charge of traffic. "Come," he waves, and the stream surges on. "Stop," he signals, and machines and men are dead in their tracks. The policeman controls the traffic, has it under his charge; he is responsible *for* it.

The other side of the meaning appears when we ask, "*To* whom is he responsible for the traffic?" And here it is that Epictetus teaches us so well. I should like to quote a famous and beautiful passage:

"But some one in authority has pronounced the sentence: 'I judge you to be impious and profane.' What has befallen you? I have been *judged* to be impious and profane. Anything else? Nothing. Suppose he had passed judgment upon the hypothetical proposition, 'If it is day it is light,' and had pronounced it to be false, what would have befallen the proposition? In this case who is judged—who condemned? The proposition, or he who is deceived concerning it? Does he who claims the power of judging you know what "pious" or "impious" means? Has he made it his study or learned it? Where? From whom? A musician would not regard him if he pronounced bass to be treble; nor a mathematician if he judged that lines drawn from the center to the circumference are unequal. And shall he who is truly learned pay attention to an unlearned man, when he pronounces upon pious and impious, just and unjust?"

Here is, I think, in clearest terms the most important meaning of "responsible to." To whom must I give account of the things under my control; who has a right to judge my work; who may rightly say whether or not my work is rightly done? To him I am responsible. To be responsible to a person means to be bound to pay regard to his appraisal of my work.

If now we compare the handling of traffic with the handling of a college, the differences of the two institutions will appear in these terms. The policeman is "responsible for" with an abruptness and arbitrariness of which faculty and president do not dream. In our realm neither men nor boys run at the beck and call of other persons. We deal not with machinery, but with meanings. Our control is a very gentle one as compared with that of the guardian of the corner of the street.

But in the other meaning the tables are reversed. Just behind the traffic despot is the sergeant; and at his shoulder, in turn, the captain; and over him, the chief. And each may say to him below, "This is the way you are to do." And afterward he says, "That was wrong; don't do that any more." Each is responsible *to* some one at his elbow or his neck. Each pays, must pay, regard to some one over him. Who plays this upper rôle in college life? "We," faculty and president, are in control. Who has a right to judge our work and ask of us regard for his appraisal? To whom are we responsible? This is the question of our paper.

I have in mind to consider a list of answers commonly given to this question. These answers fall into two groups. In advance of the discussion of them may I urge again that the special meanings of our terms should be kept clearly in mind and that others should not be allowed to take their places. Perhaps I should also ask that the attempt to be at once clear and brief in dealing with a confused situation should not be regarded as controversial or ungracious.

§ 2

First, then, *are we responsible to our students?* Clearly we are not. We are responsible for our students, but not to them. I do not mean that we are responsible for our students in all their characteristics and activities. There are, for example, certain enterprises which the students themselves carry on, of which they are in charge. In this field their responsibility should be as large and as free as it can be made. But in our own field, in the making and working out of plans for teaching and research, we are in control. In this field the opinions of undergraduates are always interesting and sometimes important, but they can never be decisive. We, as faculty and president, must assume responsibility for our side of the process of education. We cannot submit our judgment for confirmation by that of our students.

Are we responsible to the parents of our students? Here again the answer is negative, but not so clearly. We are responsible on behalf of parents, but not to them. Parents intrust their sons to us to be taught. If the sons are not well taught, then the parents have a right to regard us as having failed to do for them what we undertook to do. And yet the fact remains that we will not accept the judgments of parents as to the success or failure of our work. They seem to us often satisfied without proper cause and dissatisfied without reason. We will not receive boys with qualifications or directions as to how they are to be taught. Obviously enough, if parents are not satisfied, their sons may be withdrawn from our instruction. And unless parents are willing to intrust their sons to us, we shall have no pupils to teach. And yet the fact remains that unless they are really intrusted to us, unless we are given charge of the aims and methods of educational work, unless we are authorized to act on behalf of the parents in these respects, we will not accept the boys as pupils. We will take responsibility on behalf of parents only on condition that we are not held responsible to them.

Are we responsible to the public? No, most

emphatically. We are responsible in the interest of the public, but we are not submissive to its judgment concerning its own interests. No one can state too strongly the demand which may be made upon us that we be public-minded and public-hearted. But, on the other hand, no one can state strongly enough our need of independence from outside influence. More than anything else, the public interest of a democracy demands that its learning and teaching shall be free, shall not be subject to popular pressure or review. We may not be told what conclusions our study and teaching are to reach. Least of all may we be subjected to the impertinence which expects of us that we make a good impression upon people who do not understand, that we cater to their favor, that we make ourselves popular. No democracy can afford to have either its courts or its learning subject to its own whim, its caprices, its ignorance, or even its common sense. A people which is being taught may have its own opinions about its teachers, but the teachers as such may give little regard to those opinions.

Are we responsible to donors? Surely not. They make it possible for us to do our work, but in the doing of the work they have no other part. Least of all do they hold us accountable to them. No donor who understands his gift or us would wish to have it so. A donor seeks for some one competent to use his money for important ends, and having found the person or the institution which he trusts, he gives the money into its control. But if he kept control himself, he would deny the competence of those to whom the gift is made. He would be paying them to do his work, not theirs. On such a scheme our colleges would be for hire. But men or institutions which announce themselves for hire go to the highest bidder. Donors would buy the teaching which they want, and others would pay larger sums to get some other teaching done; and colleges would flourish on the money side; our salaries would rise to levels which we mention only in our dreams. Why not? Because, on such a scheme, our donors would not make their gifts; it contravenes the very purpose which they have in mind. To pay for learning which a man could get under his thumb by paying for it would be a sorry bargain. That is not what our donors give their money for. They look for men and institutions which in the very nature of the case cannot be hired, cannot be held responsible to them or to their fellow-donors.

Are we responsible to the church? Taking
higher education in the large, the church is perhaps our greatest benefactor. It has established
and nourished our older institutions of learning
and it still builds up the younger ones. Are we
therefore responsible to it? It is one of the chief
glories of the church that we are not. I do not
pretend here to speak of the theory and practice
of the Catholic communions; but of the Protestant
churches it is true that as their colleges have
gathered strength, they have been set free to do
their own work, to follow their own direction.
Here is a fine relationship. An institution
pledged to support a point of view has recognized that the learning which it needs cannot be
pledged to any point of view. Belief has welcomed criticism, creeds have demanded searching
for knowledge; faith has required that doubters
do their work with honesty and carefulness. The
church with which we have to do does not demand
support from us; it gives support to us. Whatever unruly minds within the church may claim,
whatever weak and vagrant minds within the colleges may pledge to give, both church and college
know that claims and pledges are not current coin
in such a realm. Our modern church, knowing
the modern world, may shudder at the task which

modern teachers face. It knows how great is
their responsibility. But if you ask, "To whom
are they responsible?" it will not say, "To me."
Out of its own experience in like relations it
knows better than that.

Are we responsible to our alumni? No.
Rather are they responsible to us. We have
spent ourselves in trying to reveal to them the
way of high-minded, intelligent living. Through
us, in some measure, they have had the best of
life's opportunities. We have a right to an accounting of what they have done with it. That
accounting would reveal the success or failure of
our work. If graduates are uneducated, then we
are nothing. But in many external ways the
American college has confused its graduates.
Not only has it asked for help; it has also sought
for favor. Often, and in many ways quite un-
worthy of itself, it has appealed to selfish and
silly loyalties, to provincial and stupid prejudices.
And for this "we" have had to pay. We who
are in charge of learning have often craved the
favor of men who do not care for learning, and
the result is that at times the strain of labor
under the hostile scrutiny of thousands of angry,
uncomprehending eyes becomes almost unbear-
able.

But, on the other hand, let it be said that, in
terms of its possibilities, the relation of the graduate to his college is one of the finest things in
our American social life. It can take up and
gather together thousands of men into a common
devotion to things high and fine as no other in-
stitutional relationship can dream of doing. It
may become, and I think is more and more tending to become, a genuine community of learned
living. In that community the alumni will not
hold us responsible to them. Rather, in the attempt at mutual understanding and coöperation
they will give to us the help which they have to
give, and we will share with them the responsibility which is ours to share.

Are we responsible to trustees? Legally we
are; in more essential ways we are not. Legally,
the trustees are the chartered body, possessed of
all the rights which the commonwealth bestows.
Legally, "we" are the servants of the trustees;
we are engaged by them and paid by them; we
may be dismissed by them, and in matters of policy and procedure we may be overruled by them.
And yet this legal relationship is a superficial
one. A college in which teachers were "dismissed" would be a sorry thing. A college in
which the faculty and president were overruled

on academic issues would be something other than an institution of learning.

And here it is well to remember that the granting of authority to boards of trustees as we now have them rests upon a historical confusion. The men first commissioned by states to establish universities and to care for learning were groups of scholars, and the rights and duties assigned to them were the rights and duties of scholarship. Only gradually has there grown up behind these the second group—the board of property-holders and business-managers. Legally, the powers formerly granted to scholars belong now to the "legal" board. But essentially they do not. If boards of trustees, as we now have them, were to claim in actual fact and procedure the rights and privileges granted to those in charge of scholarship, it would be inevitable that such boards should be abolished. In an age of material growth those boards have an exceedingly important secondary task to do; but the trustees who understand their task know that it is secondary rather than primary. They know that scholarship may never be made subservient to the material forces by which it is sustained.

If it should happen, as sometimes it has happened, that scholars are summoned before boards of trustees to give account of their study and teaching, then the time for revolt would have come. "We" are not in that sense responsible to trustees. Whatever their individual qualifications, trustees are not, as such, scholars. They have not the right, nor do those among them who understand claim the right, to pass upon matters of scholarship. In the last resort their task is to see to it that education is placed in the charge of men who are competent to manage it and who are therefore not responsible to them. To be a good trustee requires a high degree of imagination, a stalwart confidence in the ability of learning to care for itself. He is a wise trustee who does not take his work too solemnly.

But are we not responsible to the state? It gives us legal being and authority. May it, then, judge our work? Certainly not in any except a very narrow sense. The state makes us and it may destroy us; but if it makes us at all, it must make us free. No state is safe, either for itself or for its people, unless its basic principles as well as its customary procedure are open to the free and unhindered criticism of its citizens. And in this sense our scholars and teachers are foremost in the work of critical understanding. Every free people knows that its state is an instrument of its will which must be constantly studied and examined, which must be kept true and made even more true to the purpose which it serves. It follows that no free people will allow its state to restrain its scholars and teachers.

§ 3

In the first of our second group of answers we find the academic teacher at his worst. In it his mind and his disposition both seem at times to suffer collapse. It is the answer of stark and blatant individualism.

In the mind there is a bad argument. It says, "Since I am not responsible to student or parent, to church or donor, to public or graduate, to trustee or state, then I am responsible to no one outside myself; I am responsible to myself alone." It is a bad argument for two reasons. First, it may be that our list is not complete; there may be other objects which have claim to our regard. But, second, even if there were not, the conclusion would not follow. The phrase "responsible to myself" is a very bad phrase. Responsibility is an external relation. If there is no one or nothing outside myself to which I can be responsible, then the term responsibility

does not apply to me. If I *am* responsible, then
there is something other than myself to which I
acknowledge my responsibility. In the ordi-
nary use of terms I cannot be responsible to
myself.

And in the realm of the disposition the situation is even worse. Here men sometimes swag-
ger and are defiant. They challenge you to show
them any one to whose judgment they must con-
form. They are hard and opinionated, sometimes even unpleasant and objectionable in in-
sistence on their rights and liberties. Now and
then you find one who is much more interested
in the freedom and ultimacy of his own thinking
than in the corresponding rights of other men.
These men speak of being captains of their souls
and masters of their fates. Such teachers and
scholars are not helpful in present-day American
life. We have, without such teaching, quite
enough of the aggressiveness and self-assertive-
ness of a partly educated, externally successful
people. It ill becomes our scholars to insist upon
their own self-sufficiency. Scholars as well as
other men do owe allegiance; they are responsible. And the question still remains to puzzle
us, To whom are they responsible?

There are, I think, two relationships in which

the scholar feels and acknowledges responsibility. The first and lesser of these is the relation to other teachers and scholars, to other seekers after the truth. The second and greater responsibility is that which we feel and acknowledge toward the truth itself. In these two, so far as an answer to our question is possible at all, the answer will, I think, be found.

The lesser responsibility is immediate and certain. Every scholar has regard for the judgment of other scholars. There is a fellowship of learning in which all alike are enrolled, an enterprise of learning in which all are engaged. And in this enterprise each worker is responsible to his fellow-workers. What he may do depends upon what they have done. Upon what he does they try to build. And as they build, sooner or later they find him out. If his work is straight and true, it stands their test; if it is weak and false, they put him aside as one who has failed them in the common task. Within the fellowship of scholars each scholar is responsible.

But the second responsibility, though more remote, is still more urgent and compelling. As against the truth which scholars have there is the truth for which they strive, which never is achieved. It is in terms of this that final judgment must be given. In terms of this each man must wait assessment of his work, the measuring of the value of the thinking he has done. What have you done for truth? for knowledge? is the major question. Here is, I think, our real responsibility.

But is this truth a something other than ourselves, a something apart to which we may acknowledge our responsibility? I think it is. I think that thinking means that somehow in the very nature of the world itself there is a meaning which we seek, a meaning which is there whether we find it there or not. That meaning is the final standard of our work, the measure of all we do or hope to do or fail to do. To it we are responsible.

This meaning, which we do not fully know as yet, which we can never fully know, is not an easy thing to talk about. Just so the beauty which men have not seen, but yearn to see, the goodness which no man can reach, but which mankind must ever strive to gain, the end toward which he makes his way—these final ends elude our grasp. And yet they are in some sense real; they are outside ourselves; and being real and being what they are, they are our masters. To them we owe allegiance. To what they are we pay regard. In them we seek right judgment of ourselves. To them we are responsible.

§ 4

Through all this paper there has run, I fear, a certain seeming arrogance. Has it been assumed that "we" are not as other men are? Are scholars a special class free from the bonds which bind the common run of men? Are we peculiar? Do faculty and president really differ from the guardian of the corner of the street? No and yes.

Scholars and other artists are favored of fate. They are the fortunate ones of human circumstance in that they work with love of what they do. Over against them are the artisans whose work is done not for itself but for the sake of pay or something else external to the work itself. And out of these two groups there come two different kinds, two different measures of responsibility.

But we have made the line too sharp. All men are artists in some region of their living—the regions where they really live. Life is essentially an art. Policeman or professor, all men are doing acts for which they are not paid, for which no pay is possible. Men smile or frown, have faith

and courage or fail to have them, love fineness,
order, meaning, fitness, reverence, friendliness,
fairness, or fail to value them. And in this
world of things we care about, policemen and
scholars are alike in their responsibilities. Each
feels a sense of kinship with the other men who
share his values, a sense of the necessity of
"playing the game" with them. And all together are alike submissive to the world whose
values master them, the world they serve. For
every man this is the field of conscience, of freedom, of worship, of final values.

But, with respect to work, men fall apart as
we have said. For most of us work is for pay.
And if the pay were stopped, the work would
stop as well. To workers in this field some one
has said, "If you will do this thing you do not
wish to do, then I will give you something which
you want." So is a bargain made. And when
this offer is accepted, one takes responsibility in
a special sense. One has agreed that, for a consideration, he will do the will of some one else.
It is agreed that he who gives the pay shall say
what he wants done and how it shall be done;
and we who take the hire must give regard to
what he says. The bargain is that we shall be,

so long as we are in it, responsible to him who pays the wages.

But, with respect to work, scholars and other artists are a special, fortunate class. They work, but no one tells them how it must be done. Even in their work they have the greatest blessing which a man can have—freedom to do the thing that seems to him worth doing. And they must be responsible not to the men who pay them, but only to the causes which they choose and to the men who work beside them. Their work and worship coincide.

To be a scholar or an artist is to work directly for the things you care about. Such men do not escape responsibility; rather they welcome it and will not give it up. Their duty is to care about the things for which they work—and, if a conflict comes, to care for nothing else.

IS OUR WORLD CHRISTIAN?

BACCALAUREATE SERMON, 1923

IS OUR WORLD CHRISTIAN?

MEMBERS of the class of 1923: On this last Sunday of your college course, I should like to talk with you about the things which you have heard said from this pulpit on the Sunday mornings of these four years. I cannot, of course, take up with you all the themes to the discussion of which we have together listened. There is, however, one central theme which has dominated all the rest. Over and over again our preachers have tried to tell us, as they have eagerly tried to see for themselves, just what it means to call our mode of life in America a Christian way of living. The modern preacher, as we have seen him, is ever at the question. What do you mean, what ought you to mean, by the phrase, a Christian life, a Christian civilization? It is this theme concerning which I should like to have our last talk together.

We shall not hope, of course, to find a ready and easy answer to our question. It is a question which every civilization asks and which no civilization ever fully answers. Men do not know themselves nor do communities. Forever in the past, as forever in the future, scholars and teachers and preachers are given the task of finding what men are. What are we in ourselves? What do we really want; what do we value; what do we think; what do we intend? The human mind has mastered many mysteries; the riddles of the outer world are daily solved by clear and sharp technique. But what is man? That question is not answered. Rather it seems that each discovery of the outer world obscures the inner, leads men astray still further from themselves. As man controls the world, he seems to lose himself. I only say he "seems." Perhaps it would be truer to say, "The greater man's achievement, the more he has to understand." But whether that be true or not, our question in its modern form is not any easy one; we shall not quickly find an answer.

There are two questions concerning Christianity, each important enough in itself, upon which I cannot touch in this brief paper. I shall not ask, by way of history, just what was said two thousand years ago, by whom and when and in what circumstances. The studies of textual criticism, as touching upon the sayings of Jesus,

I do not know. Nor do they fall within my present mood. So, too, I do not wish to measure the Christian creed in terms of other creeds, to show it better or worse than all the other beliefs which foreign peoples have made the bases of their living. In place of queries such as these, I plan to take our common moral teaching, just as we find it in ourselves, in you and me and all of those around us. If you and I are Christians, then what is Christianity?

There is one saying of Jesus which I, at least, find very startling as we face our question. "My kingdom is not of this world," he says. "If ye love me, ye are not of this world; I am not of this world." What does he mean? Here is a dualism quite foreign to the spirit of our question. We have asked, "In what sense is our world Christian?" And Jesus seems to answer, "In no sense at all." Christianity is not a principle of civilization; it is not a theory by which this world lives. It is a criticism of this world and its theories; it is a condemnation both of civilization and of the men who make it. In what sense is civilization Christian? Apparently there is a prior question.

May I stop here a moment to remark to you, as I have often done before, how altogether

delightful are the sharpness and subtlety with
which the founder of Christianity draws his lines
and marks his boundaries? He is not looking for
numbers as he speaks of admission to his kingdom; he is talking of fitness. And the requirement seems to be that if one would choose to go
with him, then one must choose to leave this world
behind.

I have said that the judgment of Jesus upon
the world in which he lived was clear and sharp.
But it was also tragically true that the judgment
of the world upon him, though not so clear, was
quite as sharp and very quickly effective. Only
for two or three years was he allowed to have
his say and then they nailed him to a cross and
left him there to die. The world in which he
lived hated and feared him; it felt his condemnation and resented it; having the power, it killed
him. And Jesus said that those who followed
him would share that hatred. And what he said
has proved itself to be the truth. The world to-
day in its own way would do again just what it
did two thousand years ago. It fears and hates
the spirit which sees how false and futile it is.
And so it carries on its deeds of futile, silly
cruelty.

But now I am sure that you are asking questions. What is this dualism of world and other world? What does it mean to set aside this actual life of ours in favor of a different life, a life perhaps not actual? You know as well as I that men have wrought this notion into many different forms, have sought escape from life by many strange bizarre contrivances. And we who live by common sense have laughed at them and their contrivances. They seem so silly and impractical. And yet I venture to suggest that on the whole they have the truth in greater measure than the run of modern men. St. Simon on a pillar all the day, thinking of God and man! A curious way to spend one's life, we say. But what of men who spend their lives in trying to raise the price of what they have to sell, in trying to get as much and give as little as they can? That is, it seems to me more tragic than being a saint against the sky. St. Simon's life is not as bad as life can be.

And yet the ascetic scheme, as men have practised it, does not, so far as one can see, give us our answer. Jesus did not withdraw from life. He taught and healed and preached and had good fellowship. What did he mean by living in another world? I think you see his meaning most clearly in the men he chose as enemies, the men whom he attacked. He was not hard on sinners. He scarcely mentions doubters or disbelievers. His chosen enemy was the Pharisee, the man whom men call good, the man who makes and keeps intact the social order of the time. If we could understand his horror of these, and of their world, I think that we would get a glimpse of what he means, would sense his yearning for another world.

What does he say of Pharisees? What is his charge against them? It was that they were hypocrites. They seemed to him to say the words but not to do the deeds. They loved to be seen of men as righteous, but in their hearts it was the being seen and not the righteousness which moved them. And Jesus said, "Not every one that saith unto me, Lord, Lord, shall enter the kingdom of heaven, but he that doeth the will." They knew the law which Jesus preached and slipped it easily from off their tongues, but in their lives it was not law; rather it was denied and set aside. To say and not to do—that was the thing which Jesus hated, the thing that seemed to him to make this world a sorry, dreadful place from which one must escape if one could live at all.

I wonder if we can put this feeling into modern

terms, can find hypocrisy among ourselves to-day, can feel the dualism that seemed two thousand years ago to tear the world apart. What does it mean to be a hypocrite? What does it mean to have a principle upon our lips but quite a different principle controlling what we do? Is it so bad that nothing could be worse? I think it is. To say what life should be, and then to make it something else—that breaks our human task in two; that is destruction of man's work; it is the spirit's death.

I hope that you will join me, giving me all the patience that you have, as I attempt to make this statement less abstract, to put it into modern terms. There are two aspects of our human nature to which I must appeal. The first has to do with the relation of principles to practice. It says that every principle, before its work is done, its meaning realized, must find its way into the field of practice, must be a principle of action. The second statement is that human nature is self-critical. Man does not simply act; he measures his acts, measures himself; stands off and criticizes what he does and what he has not done. I wish that we might make these statements clear and telling.

If the first statement is true, then, in the last

resort, all human questions are reduced to one, "What shall I do?" At every moment of our lives action awaits our choice, decision faces us. Habit and thought, feeling and meditation, these are our ways of seeing what the act should be. When life is difficult we cease from action for a time to search our minds, to search the world, to make a plan so that the action may be good instead of bad. Thinking in all its forms is action in suspense. It is the search in abstract terms for principles, to see the way to go, and then to go that way—that is the life of man. Man is the animal who sees his way, can tell the better from the worse and so can choose the better path.

But if man sees the way and does not go; if he has found a principle and does not follow it— what shall we say of that? If that occurs, then life is broken in two. I know that you will ask me whether a man can really see the way and fail to follow it. And I should answer no, not if he really sees the principle in all its meaning for the action which he has in mind.

But men do not see all the meaning of the thoughts they have. There is a sense in which men do take principles, do claim them as their own, and yet deny them in their acts. The man who prayed and thought through all his prayer,

"How well I pray?"—that man to Jesus was anathema. The words of holiness were on his lips, the vision before his eyes. And all that he could see and hear was just himself. "Lord, Lord!" he said, and thrilled at his own piety.

Here is, I am sure, the break in human nature that brings the prophets to despair. They give men principles by which to live and men transform them into shibboleths instead of rules of action. Men cry aloud in praise of freedom, and murder those who will not join the cry. Men dream of insight, and shut their eyes in blind intoxication of the joy of being wise. Men talk of love of man for man, and hate the man who will not share the talk. When deeds belie our words, when even the very saying of the words themselves belies the meaning which they bring, then life is cut in two, a gulf is fixed, and we must speak of "world" and "other world" and make our choice between them.

The second principle has to do with criticism. It finds in every man dissatisfaction with himself, with what he is and does. All men make judgments on themselves. And so do all communities. They look upon themselves and see their customary modes of action, their thoughts, desires, affections, choices, outward acts. And

then they say, "That was not good, but this was
better"; "life should be made like that"; "this
way that I can see is better than the way that I
have tried before." The greatest moral fact in
human nature is just this power to criticize ourselves, to view the thing we do in contrast with
the things which better thinking shows we ought
to do. Man is reflective; he is the one self-
criticizing animal. He is a spirit.

And in the larger living of communities, of
civilizations, the prophets have as special task
this work of criticism. They are the moral
critics. They stand apart from codes and institutions, from the established practices of men.
They judge those practices in terms of principles
which somehow prophets see. To see them is to
be a prophet. And then they cry aloud that institutions must be changed, that certain practices
must cease, that certain visions must be followed.
And when men hear the cry they turn to follow it. But here, alas! there often comes the
break that makes the prophet weep. On Sunday
men gather to hear the message told; they take
it to their hearts while Sunday lasts; but Monday
comes and men are at their week-day ways again.
If only they would say the vision is not true, the
prophet might reply, might join them with him

in the search for truth. But no, they say, "How beautiful a truth that is!" And then the customary way asserts its claim; the habits which are "common-sense" resume their strong command; the world goes on; and prophets, in despair, cry out in longing for another world.

You will recall that thus far I have been trying to get the sense of what a moral teacher means by "world" and "other world." We saw that Jesus found a chasm fixed in human nature, and found it at the point at which his teaching came in touch with human life. He preached a vision of what our life might be. And men about him, having seen the vision, turn back to dull, unseeing life again. That was his tragedy.

Before attempting a further statement of this situation in terms more nearly applicable to our daily life, may I try in very brief and halting words to indicate some features of that teaching which Jesus brought, concerning which he had his disillusionment. I cannot attempt to give the teaching as a whole. I shall speak only of three doctrines which Jesus preached. I give them in order that we may come into closer contact with his spirit and so may realize that attitude toward the world which mastered him. I ask you as I state these principles to do two things:

first, try to get the doctrine in itself; and, second, try to see whether or not within our modern world the doctrine is observed. Do we accept these principles and do we fail to make them do their work?

Jesus said, "Thou shalt love thy neighbor as thyself." And men agreed. I need not stop to try to say just what it was to which they gave assent. But did they cease from hate? And what of us? We, too, accept the principle and teach it to our children. But do we practise it? Yes, in a measure we do, but only in a measure that seems quite pitiful in contrast with the vision of what might be done. We live in luxury and ease while others starve. We fight like beasts of prey when interests clash; we have made the Western world just now a place of bitter, hopeless, grinding hatreds. Is this the world of which we speak when we describe ourselves as Christians?

And again Jesus said to a fine, high-minded young fellow who came to him asking what he should do, "Go sell all that thou hast and give it to the poor." And it is recorded that the young man went away sorrowful, for he had great possessions. Jesus was telling men that unless the desire for possessions is mastered and curbed by other interests, unless possessions are kept in their proper place as the mere tools and machinery of life, they will destroy the spirit which they ought to serve. And is it true to-day? What are men fighting about? What do they want? You know as well as I that men have gone possessions-mad. The modern world cries "more" and "more" and "more." The mania for making things has come upon us. We think that if machines and men can only make enough, then men, each man will have enough to satisfy him. But any one can see that as we make more things we, by the very process, make desires as well. And our desires outstrip our making of the things to satisfy them. Are we in mastery of our possessions?

And Jesus said, "I came that ye might have life and have it more abundantly." No one could doubt the rightness of that teaching. And yet men tried to shut him in, to bind him down by stiff and harsh conventions. He found one Sabbath day a poor man suffering and crippled. And the story tells us that, having compassion upon him, Jesus healed him. And pious people said, What sacrilege! How sinful! Then Jesus turned in flaming scorn on them. "I know," he said, "just where your piety stops. If one of the animals you own had fallen into a pit you would not hesitate to lift him out on the Sabbath day. It would, of course, be impious to give him Sabbath help to ease his suffering. But you are not controlled by motives such as that. You help him out because he is your property; and saving one's property is always right.''

Jesus, so far as one can see across the years, believed in life and loved it, believed in men and wanted them set free. His was no timid, petty spirit hiding from life, seeking for safety, escaping evil by eschewing good. When sinners came to him he made them feel how much he liked them. I wish the younger people of this present day could see him as I think he was. He was like them, in fierce revolt against negations. He wanted life to be itself. He knew, like them, that it is very much and very needlessly denied. He wanted life affirmed; he wanted men to be themselves; wanted to be himself; wanted that every other man should have a chance to be himself. He wanted human life fulfilled with its own beauty and significance.

But now the time is getting short. Soon, very soon, you will be marching out with your diplomas in your hands; you will have graduated. Before we let you go I must attempt to gather up the scattered threads and try to spin them together into a single strand.

Is our world Christian? I am inclined to answer yes and no; to say, it is, but, also, it is not. And yet I think a truer answer can be given. I think that in the only sense in which such men as we can take a moral creed we do accept the Christian teaching. In this we do as Buddhists do, and as Mohammedans. We take the teaching as our goal but fall far short of reaching it in acts, in working principles. And this is not an accident which comes from our peculiar weakness. It is the fate of every man, of every people. It is the essential quality of human living. Forever there is fixed in man the gulf which Jesus found. Forever men are torn asunder in just the way that we have found ourselves to be. May I explain—and then my sermon will be done?

I have complained against the world that Jesus was killed by it as soon as people thought they knew what he was teaching. And yet the selfsame world has kept that teaching in its mind, has talked of him and of his words for these two thousand years, has thought of him more than of any other man whom it has known. What shall we say of such a funny, baffling world as this—a world that slays a man, just as the Greeks slew Socrates, and then defines its very mind and spirit in terms of him?

The answer to the riddle lies in the very nature of a man. We are not one but two. Much of our modern thinking about men is over-simple in its explanations. Man is by nature of the type of a dilemna. He is himself, but also he can think and plan about himself. And thought is foreign to the nature which it thinks about. So man is foreign to himself. In many ways, of which I must not stop to speak just now, thought is abstract; it leaves the vivid actual concrete world of things and human situations; it deals with principles and universals. By means of these men hope to change themselves, or, as they said in olden days, to save their souls. Man by his thought, his insight, is leading, dragging up from out the depths himself. And though it is himself who leads, he follows most reluctantly.

At every step along the road which men have trod, the hill which they have climbed, there has been conflict. Always the men of active type, the man of "common sense," believes that he has reached the goal. This is the place, he thinks where men should live, where they should settle down, master the country, reap its fruits, and live their lives in peace. But always men have

found that in the spirit of man there is no peace
in this inactive sense. The man who does not
climb slips back. Nothing can be more clear
than that a thought accepted, put in action, and
kept free from criticism, becomes with every day
less true, less vital—becomes more false. A
thought believed and only that, becomes un-
worthy of belief. And so man ever goads himself again to travel the unending road. His life
is not a state; it is a process.

And now before I say my final word to you
we must return again to talk of Pharisees,
to try to do them justice. They are the
men whom critics criticize. That is their function. They represent the action in our common
life. They make the world go round; they make
the institutions run; they get things done according to the wisdom which the past has given. And
meanwhile other men, so-called reformers, find
fault with what they do—and there is fault
enough to find.

But are they made of different stuff—these
two? Is one side right, the other wrong? May
one of them destroy the other from the earth,
sweep it aside and take the world in charge? I
do not think so. Both groups are men, and every
man has both these attitudes within himself. To

make our life complete each side must play its
part. I know reformers who complain with bitterness because men will not change the world
at once as they demand. They seem to me to
argue in this vein, "I wish to differ from every
other man and yet I ask that all the other men
should see that I am right—and do it quickly."
I often wish they had, or, shall I say, I often wish
we had a better sense of humor.

But what of Pharisees again? They are the
men of "common sense." I wish they had more
sense, could see more clearly the need of criticism
of what they do. I wish that both these groups
could see how silly and futile each would be without the other. And yet it will not do to wish too
hard, to set one's heart on having peace, the
peace that comes with understanding. These
two will never understand each other. Our
human life will never understand itself. But it
will always try; and as it tries it will succeed.
But if it stopped from trying, the human spirit
would be dead.

Members of the graduating class: I have
tried in these last words to tell you of the road
that you must go. I send you out, not in search
for things that men can own, but in the search
for self, for your own lives, and for the lives of

other men. I charge you that you seek to find
what human life can be, and that you make the
search with high intelligence and sober common
sense. You will not reach the goal. Your life is
stretched between the best that lies behind and
the achievement still before of which each vision
that we get seems only a glimmer of the truth
that men will some day win. I bid you as you
go keep fellowship with other men; no matter
what they do, no matter what they say or think,
they are your fellows in the common task. You
should regard them as you do regard yourself.

I have no fear of your discouragement at what
I have said. You do not dread the unending
road. What I do fear for you is just that leth-
argy of spirit that cuts man's life in two, that
lets our double nature fall apart. Beware of
that. We send you forth on high adventure.
This college loves the life of man, and it has tried
to make you ready for that life. Go forth and
play your part, and be you worthy of the college
which has tried to teach you how to play.

A LEADER IN FREEDOM

READ AT BROWN UNIVERSITY, MAY, 1918

A LEADER IN FREEDOM

I WONDER what Andrews would have said had he been here to-night. If for the moment he were back among us, having taken on, let us suppose, another personality, what would he say about that fellow Andrews whom we are here to honor? I do not think he would have mourned. Andrews was not a mourner before the eyes of men. He might have talked about the common tragedy of life, the life which brings us to our friends, makes us of them, so mingles us into their thoughts, their feelings and desires that they are we and we are they, and then rends us asunder in their death. And yet I do not think he would have spent his interest even upon this universal tragedy. In spite of all the richness of his feeling there was a cool impersonality about him. That you and I must die—that's in the game; and Andrews had the sportsman's instinct for playing the game just as he found it, according to the rules.

He preached in 1882 a sermon in memory of

Mrs. Mary Jane Perrin, one of his friends.   And
as he understood the task, two things he set himself to do, "to speak the simple truth about her
life," and then "to ponder long the lessons and
memory of such a life in order to be braced, for-
tified and inspired to imitate its virtues."   I
think that we may take these aims to be our own
and try to do for him what he, on like occasion,
did so gallantly for one whose quality he wished
to honor.

What is the simple truth about Andrews?   My
impression is that no one in the last half-century
has so captivated, so dominated an American
college community as he did.   How did he do it?
Or rather, how did it come about?   For no one
would ever think that he desired or planned to be
a captivator.   What was there in him that
mastered us, mastered both work and play,
teachers and students alike, that made us all his
men in everything we thought or did?   I do not
think it was primarily affection, though that was
very deep.   It was not simply pride in his
achievements, though they were great.   I know
it was not blind acceptance of his point of view;
blindness in any form was not acceptable to him,
nor, may I say, to us.   What was it, then?

I find my own answer in the words of Epicte-

tus the Stoic as he tells of his admiration for
Socrates, his spiritual master. In a splendid
passage he contrasts the regard which men have
for tyrants with that which they have for leaders. "Who pays regard to you as to a man?" he
asks the tyrant. "Who would wish to be like
you, who would desire to imitate you as he would
Socrates?"

It was, I think, something of the regard which
free men paid to Socrates, their master, that we
have paid to Andrews. "Who pays regard to
you as to a man? Who would wish to be like you,
who would desire to imitate you, as he would
Socrates?" There are other men to whom we
pay greater regard as scholars, other men who
have more sharply determined the course of educational theory and practice in the country, other
men who have had a more compelling influence
upon the affairs of state; and yet in human power
to win discipleship from those about him, to make
them will to be men like him, he was unequalled.
There seemed to be in him a certain contagious
humanness that swept into the veins of other men
who felt his touch. He was, like Socrates, a
teacher in this deepest sense. You might or
might not learn from him your politics, your art,
your creed, and yet he seemed to give an answer

to that question in which all other questions are summed up, What shall I be? Some baker can tell us how to mix our bread, some soldier how to kill our foes, some artist how to paint, some gang-boss how to wield the pick and spade, but in the doing of them all there is a common human quality which may be high or low, may be the sort of thing a man should try to be, or, on the other hand, the thing men hate or ought to hate; in any one of them a man may be a man or be a cad. It was the lesson of being a man and not a cad that Andrews taught, as Socrates of old taught his Athenian boys.

What was the secret of it all? What was the quality in Andrews from which contagion of manly virtue sprang, which seemed to wind men up, to set them going at double speed when he had touched them? I think he had an extra portion of the very quality of life itself. We human beings go about our joys and tasks, pursue our pleasures, meet our obligations, passing from day to day as days go by until the end. How much of spirit is there in us for the game, for joys and pains, achievements and adventures, despairs and sharp defeats? Are we not tame and thin in spirit as compared with Andrews? He seemed to have a zest for being a man. It was not that he hoped to win; no man of sense expects too much of that. Success and failure are alike experiences of men, and in them both the spirit of a man may be expressed. It was that he had zest for life, a zest unhindered by timidity and fear, unlimited by meanness and self-seeking. He was alive and willed to be alive, and willed that other men should live; he fought with all his might against whatever threatened human life. He was a lover of mankind, not in the softer sense which runs to sentiment, but rather in a grander, savage, passionate zest for manliness, the joy of doing and seeing done the things that men may do.

One finds in many forms this zest for life which Andrews had. His humor shows it; so, too, his hatred of sham. It bubbles up in the biographies he loved to write and tell. His fearlessness that ran toward recklessness expresses it; so does his sheer democracy; and the demand he ever made for freedom for himself and other men; it is the very essence of his creed as teacher and college leader.

Never shall I forget that opening morning of the college year when out he came around the pulpit and, standing stalwart on the narrow platform, told us about Demosthenes. He loved to take a single human life and follow it. I well remember how that morning the actors in the life of Greece came forth upon the stage, and, as we followed their thoughts and deeds, how the great drama of mankind revealed itself. I have found that story again in something that he wrote four years ago, and it has still the same dramatic interest. Demosthenes and Phocion, Philip and Alexander, these were for him the men who made or marred the culture of the world. Phocion was right; Demosthenes was wrong. If Alexander could have lived another twenty years the world might have been saved from later barbarism. Greece would have conquered Asia; Asia and Greece with mingling culture would have conquered Rome; and they together, dominated by the thought of Greece, would have conquered Europe. The darkness of the early Middle Ages would never have descended on the world. Greece with its freedom and intelligence would have made the whole world free. If only Macedonia's king had lived another twenty years!

So, too, he tells the tales of other men and women, of Robert E. Lee, the blameless foe, of Christopher Columbus, self-seeker, pirate, bigot, finding a new world by mistake, and yet a mighty man who found a world because he ventured forth

when other men had only thought of venturing.
With equal zest he tells the tales of Mrs. Perrin
and of Immanuel Kant who, like Columbus, ventured forth and found or made another world for
men to live in. You who have laughed with Andrews in the past, who have enjoyed his jokes and
quips, his flashing insight into men, if you would
laugh with him again, look up the story which he
wrote of his first year's experiences as a soldier
in the Civil War. He tells of all his pals and
their adventures, of Frisbie the cook, of whom he
says: "Frisbie had not very many faults. The
only ones I can readily recall were swearing,
gambling, lying, drinking, stealing and speaking
evil of the orderly sergeant; but in these few, I
feel constrained to testify, he was an adept and
did not do things by halves." And there was
Pilkington who was in drinking more than a
match even for Frisbie. As Andrews says, "He
never allowed an opportunity for getting drunk
to pass unimproved." And Charley Schmidt and
Aleck Wilson and Jeremiah Horan, these were his
friends, and through the blackness of the first
year of war, he tells the story of their doings as
if they had been a group of boys at play.

I have not time to-night to follow into other
fields the varying expressions of that essential

quality which made him what he was. But, you who knew him, I ask you, was he not more a man than you or I? Was he not more akin to other men? Did he not love the very quality and art of being human?

But now that we have made our little formula, what does it mean? I wonder if we know. What is this humanness, this manliness of which we speak? What does it mean to be more of a man than other men, as Andrews was?

There is a very pretty fallacy which we commit as we relate ourselves to heroes, like Andrews or Socrates. It might be called the fallacy of stealing the hero; and every one of us who claims a hero as his own is likely to make the blunder.

Andrews was fond of Frisbie who excelled in getting drunk, and Frisbie doubtless felt that Andrews was a man just like himself. I have no doubt that he compared his hero Andrews with other primmer, more restricted souls, and saw that Andrews was with him, not them, that he was essentially a good fellow like himself. And he was right in part. And yet I do not think that Andrews thought that being a drunken sot was worthy of a man. I think that Frisbie, by an honest blunder in his logic, was trying to steal a

hero whom he had no right to claim. I well recall how Andrews loved a baseball game; do you
remember how he lost his self-control when Ten-
ney knocked three-baggers up the right-field line?
Andrews so loved a game that any boy who played
could feel him sharing the grand excitement of
the contest till the game was lost or won. And
yet to make of him a sport is to belittle and belie
him. He did not think that running miles or lin-
ing them out was occupation high enough for one
who had the chance of doing something more.
Andrews loved games; and yet you do not give
the essence of the man by saying that he loved
them.

And so in many other ways we might attempt to
steal our hero. But just the pity of it is that
when we steal we do not get him. The trouble is
we fail to understand him. I cannot doubt that,
like the other followers, I, too, am tempted to
commit the sin, to make the theft. Being a
teacher, I want to claim him for the teacher's
trade; being a college president, I feel the need
of some one stalwart and beloved to stand beside
me in the fight. And yet I come to you to-night
to give you his own words. I have sought through
many pages to find the things he said about himself and other men.

As nearly as I can, I wish to tell you what he says about the sort of man a man should wish to be.

Andrews believed, I think, that men are climbing up from lower things to higher, from cruder and more stupid forms of life to finer ones and better. It was that sense of human striving that made him so insistent that every man should have a chance. He hated privilege and caste, the bonds of custom and advantage that keep men tied to what they are, that keep men down and will not let them up. Always he found the world unjust to multitudes of men who never have a chance to be themselves. But quite as much, I am sure, he hated the inner bonds of men, the impotence that keeps them slack and lazy when they have a chance, the lack of zest for life's adventure that keeps them satisfied with stubble for food and dross for merchandise, that keeps the spirit dormant in its husk of flesh. He loved to see the human spirit on its way, free in the search of its adventure.

It seems to me that I have found him most fully revealed in those years in Florida when he was waiting for the ending of his time to come. What did he do?

He thought and studied and wrote. What were

his subjects? "Wealthy Men and the Public Weal" was one of them; the paper on "Greek National- ism and Home Rule in the Fourth Century B. C." from which I quoted, was another. Next came the "Renaissance"; then "Milton's Ecclesiastic- Political Setting"; and finally the study on "Art and Character" in which the deepest yearnings of the man achieved their last expression. I think we find him there perhaps as nowhere else. He thought of Art just as he thought of every other phase of human life, in terms of character. The craving for beauty he found to be not mere in- stinctive, unrelated passion, but the expression in fitting forms of all the deepest meanings, the sub- tlest treasures of the human spirit. Listen to his words as he portrays the beauties of the paradise for which he yearns:

We know the joy of gazing at great works of art. It is indescribable, giving uplift and inspiration like nothing else. Being asked where he wished to be buried, Michelangelo replied: "Where my eyes may for- ever rest on the words of Brunelleschi." He of course referred mainly to the Florence Cathedral. But more glorious far than any works of Brunelleschi or other mortal artist will be the objects on which souls who attain will have the privilege of gazing in the world where they shall be. Everywhere they will see in the spirits of just men made complete the masterpieces of

the infinite Artist, characters more splendid than any
that this life has revealed, on which none will be able
to gaze without rapture. But, best of all, they shall
see in the total there set before them, the Ideal, the
Supreme Good, infinitely perfect morally and so infinitely beautiful, the Author of all moral as of all
physical beauty, realizing beauty in absolute and in-
communicable perfection. That is what the pure in
heart shall see. That, indeed, is the chief end of man
interpreting the catechism's language, so deep with
truth—"to appreciate the Eternal in its real glorious-
ness and to enjoy the same forever."

That in his own day and place, was the spirit
and mind of Andrews as he brought his life together towards its goal. And a little later, to
speak for himself, he quotes from Emily Dickin-
son:

A Service of Song

Some keep the Sabbath going to Church;
  I keep it staying at home,
With a bobolink for a chorister
  And an orchard for a dome.

Some keep the Sabbath in surplice;
  I just wear my wings,
And instead of tolling the bell for Church
  Our little sexton sings.

God preaches—a noted clergyman—
  And the sermon is never long.

So instead of going to heaven at last
  I 'm going all along.

But you may say these were the words and
thoughts of later years when illness pulled him
down. I do not think that illness ever pulled him
down. What was he in his active years; what did
he do and wish to do when he was here at Brown?
I think that Andrews was by instinct and conviction a scholar and a teacher. He thought of
scholarship as guiding and directing human life,
and so he flung himself with all his might into its
conflicts and called on other men to come with
him and take their places in the fray. His life
was far too busy, far too much concerned with
other men and their affairs, to let him take the
place he might have won in scholarship. And
yet I think that both by instinct and achievement
he far surpassed the other men who had a corresponding place and opportunity. We knew him
as our guide and teacher, the builder of a faculty,
the man who took a college into his hands and
made it brim with life and vigor, the man to whom
trustees and students, teachers and graduates,
friends and foes alike, all turned their eyes. He
was for us a busy man, a great administrator.
What do you think he would have said about himself? I know that in the eight short years he

spent at Brown he published more studies and
books than most men of his trade can publish in
a lifetime. I had almost said more books than
many of them can read within a lifetime. Somehow or other, this man whom we interpreted in
terms of action was finding a quiet place where he
might read and think and write. How was it that
he brought and kept the faculty that clustered
round him here? Because they knew that he was
one of them. Do you think they stole their hero?
One of them said to me a little while ago, one of
the greatest teachers that this college has ever
had, "He [Andrews] gave to me as no one else
has ever done the sense that men must know and
understand; he sent me on intoxicated with desire
for truth." Yes, Andrews had the passion for
the scholar's life; he had as well the zest for work-
manship that brought men to him and swept them
on beside him in the game. In those eight years
that he was here at Brown as president, he published, besides the many sermons and addresses
that he gave, besides the lecture outlines that he
made in several fields of philosophic thought, besides translations from Droysen in history and
Paulsen in philosophy—besides all these and new
editions of his earlier works, he published as
books, "An Honest Dollar," "Wealth and Moral

Law," "History of the United States," and "History of the Last Quarter Century of the United States." How did he do it? Nothing but sheer capacity for life, nothing but passionate finding of life in books could have sustained him through the labor that he undertook. For him his books were just the weapons of a man.

This was the man who came to Brown in 1889 as president. I need not tell again the story of the things he did. That story has been often told and will be often told again. All that I care to say just now is this: he mastered us—his scholars. He had a purpose that we felt, a grip on human life that caught us fast; we got the sense that in a college such as Brown there was a mighty something to be done, that he was doing it, and we must join him in the task. What was the thing he wanted done? He put it clearly enough in papers and addresses, inside the college walls and outside as well. He always said, when called upon to explain the college, that its aim was first of all a moral aim. Always he said that scholarship and learning, teaching and study must be used for making character, for making men. And we applauded to the echo. "Yes, yes," we said, "he is no pedant, no bookworm, no idle theorizer; he does not care how much

you know; he only asks the kind of man you are."
And all the time in our enthusiasm we were denying every word he meant to say. He meant that
colleges should take their books and by their
books should make boys into men. We all too
often thought he meant to say, "Character is
better far than books; if only one decides to be
a man, shoves out his chest and says, I am a
manly man, it makes no difference whether he
thinks or not." But Andrews had his view of
what a man should be, of what he might be made
when culture, its learning and its art, its literature and thought, its science and religion, had
had their way with him. He dreamed of making
men of culture; we all too often thought he
planned to make the sort of men we were.

I am not here complaining especially of the
men of Brown. In every other college of this
unenlightened land of ours this drama has been
played. But I do know that Andrews had the
sense of bitter disappointment in the results of
college teaching. It was this, I think, which
drove him in 1897 to plan for having a part in
that great college of the common people which
the "Cosmopolitan Magazine" had undertaken.
It found expression later when he said that he
would much prefer to be a teacher in the common

schools rather than in a college. In 1904, speaking at a convention of his fraternity, he made his theme "The Decline of Culture," and after sharp and biting criticism of college teaching, he said:

No wonder that students in college now show, as compared with those of years past, great dearth of moral enthusiasm. There is fair zeal for hard study, for intellectual attainments, for qualifications that shall bring place and name and fortune; but little for ideals, truth on its own account. Quite in vain, I think, would you search American institutions of high learning to find students, as one could easily do once, in societies, in dormitories, on college walks, engaging each other with blood-heat arguments, sometimes leading to duels, on questions like slavery, capital punishment, the rights of majorities. Equally vital questions crowd the forum to-day, issues on whose solution the whole weal of humanity hangs; but they stir very little the breasts of college men. Nor can I refer this in any great degree to change of view touching debate as a means of advancing truth. Its main cause is sheer moral apathy.

And then again in closing, quoting from Emerson, he said:

Brothers in Delta Upsilon, trebly loud, earnest and numerous since the day of Emerson's warning, "You hear on every hand the maxims of a low prudence. You hear that the first duty is to get land and money, place and name. 'What is this truth you seek? What is this beauty?' Men will ask with derision.

"Be bold, be firm, be true. When you shall say, 'As others do, so will I. I renounce, I am sorry for it, my early visions; I must eat the good of the land and let character-making go until a more convenient season'—then dies the man in you; then once more perish the buds of nobility, piety, and truth as they have died already in a thousand thousand men. The hour of that choice is the crisis of your history. . . . Bend to the persuasion which is flowing to you from every highest prompting of human nature to be its tongue to the heart of man and to show the besotted world how passing fair is wisdom."

Men of Brown, we had a prophet here among us, and we followed him, or thought we did. But like the followers of many another prophet, we did not always understand the message that he brought. We paid regard to him as to a man; we wanted to be like him; we willed to imitate him. Yes, but did we not steal our hero, each for himself? Did we take pains to know him as he was? No man may claim to be his man, to walk with him, who spends his days in idleness or sloth; nor may a man who, seizing some advantage which the Fates have furnished him, live by the labor of the hands of other men; nor may a man who hinders other men from rising up to be the men they might become; nor may a man who shrinks and trembles in the face of life; nor may a man who does not know the joy and sustenance of books that tell what human living is; nor may a man who does not live in yearning adoration of the beauty of the world; nor may a man who has not in him the longing to find that which a man may worship as his God. These were the things that Andrews found in human life; these make the humanness that we have felt in him. We may not shout for him unless we shout for them.

Dear, gallant, stalwart, splendid Bennie Andrews. The zest of life was in him to the brim. He loved the things a man might be. Oh, what a gallant fight he made, and what a hard one! I cannot mourn that he is gone; I am too glad that he has been and is. He was a man. Yes, take him all in all, we shall not see his like again.

WHAT ARE COLLEGE GAMES FOR?

"The Atlantic Monthly," November, 1922

WHAT ARE COLLEGE GAMES FOR?

THERE is one obvious outstanding fact about the younger generation, viz., that the older generation made it. The marks of its makers are upon it. These young people who torment us, who baffle us, who seem so different from ourselves—these are our children. Whatever they are they owe to us. We gave them birth; we gave them training; we gave them the social order which shapes and fashions them. If they have virtues, the cause is in us; if they have vices, it is we who brought them into being. In every proper causal sense they are ours. If then we wish to understand our children we must examine ourselves. If we would prescribe for their diseases or cultivate their virtues, we must find the sources of these in ourselves and in our world. Just as the fathers, whom we approve, made us, so we made these who follow us, whom we often condemn. But the approval on the one hand and the disapproval on the other seem to clash when they meet together in us who stand between.

Why so ill an effect from so good a cause?

The principle just stated holds good, I think, for many present situations. But more specifically, for our immediate purpose, it throws light upon what is known as the Athletic Situation in the Colleges. It may be worth while to discuss that situation in the light which the principle will give.

A few days ago, the postman brought us a letter of a type which is fairly familiar. It reads as follows:

Sept. 5, 1922.

DEAR SIR: I would like to enter Amhurst College, on behalf of my athletic ability. I have played football for the past five years. I played three years for —— High School, selected in —— all scholastic team in 1919. I have been a scrubb at —— College for the past two years. One varsity season under —— and the other in my freshman year. My weight at present is 165 lbs. and play the position of an end. I also participate in baseball.

My past record at —— is highly graded due to my boxing ability. I boxed the past two seasons for —— Varsity. I realize the fact that your College does not have this sport, but I do promise to make good on my football ability. I would like to hear from you at your earliest convenience, anytime before your registering days or the first day of school.

I would gladly except your most legitimate offer towards a scholarship in helping me get an education.
Very truly yours,

___ ___

Now in the spirit of our principle we are bound
to ask, "What have we done to deserve this?"
Here is a young man rejoicing in the fruits of two
years of teaching in a well known American college. Presumably he has been under the instruction of school and college for fourteen or fifteen
years. Presumably his achievements have been
accepted as sufficient basis for promotion by
school and college throughout that period. And
yet he is apparently untouched by what a school
or college ought to give. And this appears at
two points. First, he cannot write an English
sentence. If his skill in athletics were equal to
his skill in English composition, what chance
would he have of making the team? With such
equipment a football coach would look upon him
as kindly as upon a man with wooden legs or
bereft of both his arms. Upon the field men must
have speed and strength and wits; and they must
show that everything they have is forced up to
its highest point by constant, faithful practice.
But in the world of books, what are the standards?
This case suggests that in the training of the

mind standards are very low compared with those which dominate the training of the body. If so, who is at fault; what can be done to clear away the fault?

And, second, the writer of this letter offers services for sale. "What will you pay," he asks, "if I will come and play upon your teams?" There is a blunder in his mind when he asks such a question: what is it? No one can blame him for offering services for sale. We all do that who earn our livings. The blunder lies in thinking that any proper college would buy such services. He thinks of us as hiring teams, as paying men to "represent" the college in its games. Who taught him things like that? Where did he get his notion of what a college is, and what a game, and what a football fight between two groups of undergraduates? Some one has led him astray, has robbed him of the meaning of college sport. Who is the guilty person? We need to fix the guilt because such robbery, such spoiling of our college games must stop. And we can stop them only by finding out just what they are and how they come about. Somewhere in what we are, in what we have done or left undone, in what we think and feel and teach, the cause of our vexation will be found. And we must search until we find it. Then having found it we must act accordingly.

§ 1

I have said that the truth about our college games needs to be discovered and stated. May I add that it should be stated very carefully? The truth is, I think, that our athletic situation is fundamentally dishonest. But "dishonest" is a dangerous term. It needs to be defined.

This charge of "dishonesty" is very commonly made just now, especially by younger people, against all our established institutions. And, in large measure, I think, the so-called revolt of youth is based upon this charge. Older people seem to say one thing when they mean another, to give one reason for an action when they are really moved by another. How much of truth is there in the charge? Is the management of the world just now unusually dishonest? Or is the resentment against dishonesty unusually keen? Both factors, I think, enter into the situation.

Men have always been moved by more than one motive at a time. And they have always been tempted to show one motive to one person and a

second motive to another in order to secure the
favor of each for a common cause. When men
say that trade follows the flag, they hope to link
together, sometimes in strange conjunctions, both
patriots and money-makers. When they add that
trade follows the missionary, they are seeking to
add religious people to the combination, or vice
versa. And the creation of just such connections
is sometimes called administration. Are we unusually clever in such duplicity or multiplicity
just now? Many younger people think we are—
and they hate it. My own observation is that
we are at present unusually mixed up by a complicated world. We have more motives to cor-
relate, more interests to manage than we are
ready for. And I doubt very much whether the
younger generation in the same situation would
have done any better with it than we have done.
But, however that may be, the two elements in
the situation seem to me to stand out with striking clearness. First, we have had in our world—
and still have—perplexities and hesitations and
concealments and devices. And second, out of
these has come a hatred of them, a demand for
straightforwardness in motive and action.

If that demand can be met without breaking
the social machinery, the younger people will

have a better world in which to live than had their elders. If they can get it they are welcome to it even though they state their discovery of it in terms of a condemnation of those who have made their achievement necessary but who also have made it possible. If they succeed they will record us as "dishonest." Perhaps a more sympathetic judgment would call us "complicated."

§ 2

Now this general social situation is strikingly illustrated in the field of college games. College sport has been mixed up with other college interests, has been administered in connection with other college enterprises, has been used for other purposes. What it needs is just to be freed from this mixture. It must be made and kept pure sport, played for its own sake, and for nothing else.

The mixture of which I speak appears in the letter which is our text. The writer hopes for a chance to play. But he also hopes for payment in return for good playing. He thinks that, for some ulterior reason, we of the college want and need good playing, and are therefore willing to pay for it. Are we? If so, why?

I should like to try to separate the original and the secondary motives which together make our complicated situation.

There are two primary motives from which college games spring, out of which the essential spirit of the games is made. The first is a desire of the players and of the undergraduate community which they represent; it is the desire for fun, for the sheer joy of competition with another college and its team. Taken all in all, there is no "outside" interest of the undergraduate years which is so compelling or, within proper limits, so worth while as this.

The second motive is the desire of players and communities for victory in the games. This, too, is essential. There can be no game without it. If one does not wish and strive for victory, then one does not play at all. To play is to play to win.

These two motives are, I think, the stuff of which college sport is made. They are not its only values, but they are, I think, its dominating intentions. Do they give us an explanation of our letter? Evidently not. Any undergraduate knows that to pay a man to play on his team is not good sport, to hire a man to be a member of the college in order that he may "represent" it, is a contradiction in terms. I do not mean to suggest that undergraduates are immune to self-contradiction. But I do think that, if undergraduates were free from our complications, they would escape this sort of contradiction. The young American is a good sport if he gets a fair chance at being one. But the sting of this letter lies in the fact that it is addressed to the college authorities, that more specifically it asks for a scholarship from the college funds as payment for athletic service. Evidently it presumes that president and faculty are interested in winning teams. Are they? And if so, why? What are their motives in relation to college sport?

My own experience in such matters has been, I think, a very fortunate one. And yet experience as well as observation compels me to give to this question an answer which one would rather not give. "We" are interested in winning teams, not only because we like to win, but also because life is easier for us, administration is more smooth, when teams are winning than when they lose. I have heard it said that the turn of a game would have much to do with the success of a drive for endowment. I have seen lists of figures eagerly compiled and scanned to show that under one administration the percentage of victories was quite as great as under another. What are the secondary motives at work here? Why does administration care for victories more than for defeats?

The answer is that victories are supposed to win for the college the favor of men who without them would be indifferent or antagonistic. To put it quite bluntly, the college needs the favor and support of men who are not sufficiently interested in its essential values to care for it because of these. It therefore makes appeal to them on other grounds. It hopes that in the fact that one football team has beaten another they will find reason for endowing the scholarship and teaching with which the first team is "connected." It offers an insult to their intelligence as an appeal to their favor.

There are two groups of men to whom this appeal is especially made, the "public" and the "athletic alumni." In the first case, it is hoped that the news of the winning of games, if properly spread abroad, will make a good impression upon people who do not know the college in other ways. In this sense, winning teams are "good advertising." It is believed that, wherever the news of victory goes, "boys" will be attracted to the college, their friends will be impressed by its strength, and so the numbers and the prestige of the institution will be increased. In the period of building up since the early nineties, this notion has been wide-spread and sometimes very powerful.

The appeal to the "athletic alumni" is very similar. These men are the graduates and non-graduates of the college who value athletic victories very highly. In some few exceedingly crude cases, they seem to care for victories and for nothing else. For these men a college is an athletic club with certain other very irritating appendages. But the greater number of the group are not so dull as this. They commonly believe, first, that victories give "good advertising," and, second, that victories indicate better than anything else the quality of the under-graduate life, and even of the college instruction and administration. For lack of other standards, they judge the college by this, with which they are familiar.

Now the essential feature of both these appeals is that the college is attempting by indirection to win the favor of men for one cause by meeting their interest in another. And this is simply one phase of the fact that those who are carrying on educational work in America must or do depend for support upon men who, in large measure, do not understand or do not care what education really is. In dealing with such men we use our games as a way of using them. It is a natural thing to do. But is it either wise or fair? My own conviction is that the procedure in all its forms is radically bad and unwise, that it defeats its own ends while seeming to gain them. In the remainder of this paper I should like to try to point out the harm which this administrative complication of motives has done to education and to the games. That it is harmful to both seems to me beyond question.

§ 3

If any one doubts that our double dealing is harmful to education, I would refer him to the letter with which this discussion began. The case is extreme but it is representative. Do we suppose that we can surround our students with a persistent and powerful misrepresentation of what they are doing in college and yet expect them to understand their task and to do it well? If we tell them that a college with good teams is a good college, what do we expect them to choose as their own college purposes? The business of "advertising" a college needs very careful scrutiny. I have yet to see any college undertake to "attract" boys by appeal to the lesser values of the college life without at the same time making it probable that the boys had better go elsewhere if they wish to get an education. We are under obligation to advertise our colleges in the sense of explaining what they are, what they have to give. But we are under even greater obligation to stop misrepresenting the college and its work in order to make it attractive to those who are not interested in it. At its best, this procedure is an attempt to catch young men unawares, to give them an education while they are thinking of something else. At its worst, it is crude and vulgar deception. But in either case it is essentially hostile to the work and the spirit of a place where learning is, where truth and knowledge are to be sought and found.

With respect to the alumni who have judged the college by its athletic victories we have, I think, genuine ground for encouragement. I say this not for administrative reasons, but because it seems to me true. Any alumnus who stops to think knows that a good team does not prove a good college. When all is said and done, it is clear that the surest and best way to get a good team is to buy it, to hire the players and to hire good coaches to train them. This has been shown very clearly in many striking cases. And in less striking cases it is equally true according to the measure of the dishonesty and lack of sportsmanship. In the face of facts like these, no one can continue to think that a college may be judged by its teams. And in general I believe that the graduates of our colleges are learning better standards, are judging not so much by petty and lesser values as by the essential things. It is at least to be sincerely hoped that this is true. Surely every president and every faculty should be busy in trying to make it true. We need from our friends, support and favor, but, far more than these, we need from our own graduates genuine and sympathetic understanding of what we are trying to do. Whatever hinders that, harms our work. Whatever increases it, makes good education more nearly possible. That athletic misrepresentation has done grievous harm to the American college, its students, its teachers, its graduates, its outside friends, no one can doubt. That it must be stopped is equally certain.

§ 4

But what harm has been done to the games themselves by the use of them for other purposes? What has administrative double-mindedness done to sport and to sportsmanship? It has not wholly destroyed them. Young men in college are still young and still men; and hence games are still games. But it has allowed the games to be shockingly changed for the worse.

When, however, one examines the damage, it appears to be due not so much to positive offenses by presidents and faculties as to the failure of these guardians of the college to take opportunities, to meet obligations with clean and decisive action. The task of understanding and placing games in the general scheme of college life is not an easy one. We have many excuses for failure to accomplish it; and yet the fact remains that we have failed, that the collegiate administration of games is on the whole a rather pitiful failure.

The difficulty of the task has arisen chiefly from the coming in of an external factor. We first thought of games as the play of students, as competition between colleges. But during the last thirty or forty years these contests have taken on very great interest for people outside the colleges. The general public, collegiate and non-collegiate, is so eager to see our contests that it is willing to pay well for the privilege. And so it has come about that more and more we have provided on our fields places for lookers-on; until now the largest "crowds" are mounting to fifties or sixties of thousands, and the gate-receipts of a team for a season may be counted by the hundreds of thousands of dollars.

Here then are the elements of a rather difficult situation. Our primary purpose is that our students play games with the men of other colleges. But other people wish to see the play and are willing to pay for the privilege. What shall we do? Shall we refuse to admit outsiders? Shall we admit them without payment? If we take payment, on what scale shall it be and what use shall be made of the money taken? Now to each of these questions our practice has given the easiest answer, whether right or wrong. If people wish to see, then of course they must be admitted. If people offer money, of course we will take it—take as much as they are willing to pay. If the money is taken in as profit from athletic games, then of course the proper use of it is for athletic purposes. These are the easy natural answers; but within them lies the cause of our disaster.

The first answer is, I think, valid. It would not be wise or friendly for us to exclude the public from our contests. From our own immediate standpoint such exclusion is desirable. If the games were not public spectacles we could have better sport, more fun, better sportsmanship than is possible with our present publicity. And yet it would be socially wrong for us to seek such seclusion. The college is, in all essential features, a public institution. Here is a "complication" from which we cannot generously or honorably escape. The public must come if they wish; and we must make them welcome, and then make the best of our situation.

The second answer is not so clearly or so completely true. I think we have a right and even an obligation to make a charge for admission to the games. It would hardly seem proper to use the funds of the college to pay for the providing of accommodations for spectators. One cannot very well use scholarship or library funds for the building of Bowls and Coliseums. But why should the charge be anything more than that of the actual additional cost of providing space and seats for those who ask us to provide them? I

can see no justification for anything more.
Surely we are not in the business of making
profits from the games of our students. Nor
are we willing that they should be in that business either. But in some way or other we have
gotten into that business, have built our fields and
used them for extracting all the money which the
traffic will bear. Here is a commercialism which
must be stopped. Young men, as well as old,
must see that it is not always necessary to take
money when it is offered. Taking money usually
implies a bargain. And in this case, the spirit
of sportsmanship stands in the way. We are
playing, not for money, but for fun.

But it is the third answer which is most clearly
and wickedly wrong. If we assume that gate-
receipts are to be charged and thereby large sums
of money are to be made available, who shall take
them? The answer given is, that if money is
made by games, it should be used for games; if
it is made by teams, it should be used for teams.
Why? What is the connection?

As matter of fact, it is the exact opposite which
is true. There can be no proper connection here.
Every one knows that in such sport as ours, the
money earned should not be given to the individual players. But it is equally true that it should

not be used for the teams. If this is done, then the winning of games and the making of money are linked together in ways which are inevitably destructive of the whole scheme of college play. If the team wins, it makes more money; if it has more money, it is more sure of winning. And so the wheel goes spinning round, and the games which we began to play for fun become great financial struggles between managers and supervisors and coaches, and scouts and other outsiders, while the players are more and more the puppets used by the machine in fashioning its successes.

Here is, I am sure, the radical blunder which has been made by our double-minded administration. We have put together play and money-making when every interest of play demanded that they be separated. When it appeared, thirty years ago, that our games were arousing public interest and could therefore be made sources of revenue, what did we say? More or less clearly two statements were made. First, this public interest, though bad for sport, is good for other reasons, and must be cultivated. And, second, the amounts of money involved are too large to be managed by undergraduates; we must establish Boards of Control to see that proper management is given. And so we took from undergraduates the management of their own games—much to their delight as they saw our more "efficient" administration. In their place we have established great systems of administration which have built Stadiums, Bowls, Coliseums, have increased gate-receipts, have aroused public interest, have "developed" teams, until the whole system has become an absurd travesty of the motive from which it sprang, the impulse of play which it was intended to serve.

Nothing seems to me clearer than that it is essential for us to cut the connection between players and teams on the one side and gate-receipts and expenditures on the other. If undergraduates wish to have games, they should furnish the players from their own ranks, should arrange their own schedules, pay their own expenses, carry on their own play. If on the other hand, people wish to come to the college grounds to see the play, the college may charge for this such payment as it thinks best. My own opinion is that it should charge the expense of the field and nothing more.

But whether the income be large or small, it should be taken and used by the college and not by the team or its management. The interests of the sport demand that the money be kept apart from it.

When one suggests that such a change as this be made, the officers of the "system" reply that under existing circumstances a change is impossible. But the officers of a system usually say that. There is no inherent difficulty in making such a change. The interests which the system is intended to serve demand that it be made.

§ 5

The absurdity of our present administration of games reaches its climax in the institution of the coach, the armies of coaches. These are men who are brought in to develop the playing skill of the team to the highest possible pitch. They are given full and complete charge of the players and the play; far more than any one else they are held responsible for victories or defeats. In return for this they are paid large, exceedingly large salaries, as judged by the standards of the college community. Now the growth of this institution is of course directly traceable to the administration of the gate-receipts. If large sums of money are available, then many and good coaches can be secured by paying for them. If good coaching is provided, the level of play is raised, more victories are won, and the gate-receipts are still further increased. The making of the money enters directly and essentially into the winning of the games. The sport is commercialized at its very center. It is not too strong a statement to say that undergraduate responsibility for the winning or losing of games has very largely disappeared.

Now here again it seems to me imperative that we go back to first principles and escape from our double-mindedness. There is no real fun, no genuine sport in hiring a man to furnish the wits, the skill, the discipline, the control by which you attempt to win a game. If undergraduates are to have real games, they must do their own coaching, take charge of their own teams, develop their own strategy, work out their own discipline; the team must be theirs, and they must win or lose on their own efforts. I know nothing more depressing than the conversation in a college community at the end of a season, when, having won or lost our games, we speculate what the result would have been, had we hired these men rather than those to take charge of the chances of victory. I am not here attacking the character or personal quality of coaches. They range in this respect from crude and vulgar outsiders to men whose friendship is gladly welcomed in any academic community. What I am saying is that with the coming in of coaching, real undergraduate competition has gone out. Students should play their own games. To see them turning to a coach who will tell them whether to hit or to wait, whether to circle the end or to plunge at the tackle—to see the giving up of the very fun of the game itself, that is a sight to make one's heart weep. It is time that we should ask, "How have we come to this?"

To the suggestion that coaches be abolished, objection has been made that "since in our intellectual work we furnish the best teaching," in the field of sports "we should give the very best teaching that there is." The objection rests, I think, on two misapprehensions. It fails to recognize the destruction of undergraduate responsibility which coaching has brought about. And, perhaps for this very reason, it hopelessly confuses "coaching" and "teaching." We have departments of physical training which are teaching in the field of athletics. And it is our hope that through them every student in the college may be given some appreciation of the joys and advantages of athletic games. But the differ-

ence between "teaching" and "coaching" is one
which no genuine teacher will allow to be ob-
scured.   The teacher develops the independence
of his pupil; the coach takes away that independence.   The teacher is preparing the pupil in general by trying to give him understanding of the
field in which his activities may lie.   The coach
is preparing him for specific tests, specific occasions, is getting him ready for a particular contest which is coming and coming soon.   For the
winning of that contest the coach takes responsibility, whether it be an entrance-examination or
a game of football.   The coach studies the actual
situation, finds out just what the factors are, determines what shall be done with respect to each,
issues his orders as to what shall be done and
what not done.   It is the business of a teacher
to develop a pupil into power and intelligence; it
is the business of a coach to win a contest.   I
know few things more amusing than a college debate in which a "coach" has told his automata
what to say.   But quite as tragic is the spectacle
of a group of boys using their arms and backs
and legs at the command of another man's wits,
and supposing at the same time that they are
playing a game.

As to the prospect of improvement here, there is some reason for encouragement. The suggestion that no one be allowed to coach unless he be a member of the faculty is being very favorably considered. It is perhaps somewhat invidious to suggest that the first step toward non-existence is membership in a faculty. But at least the suggestion does mean that we are considering the problem. My own impression is that the days of double-mindedness are going by.

§ 6

I have dealt in this paper with the effects of administration upon college games. And one does this because, after all, the attitudes and actions of faculties and presidents are the most important factors in any matter of college activity whatever it may be. That there are other sources of difficulty need hardly be said. Especially is it true that small groups of undergraduates and, more often, of graduates, with no proper sense of what a game is, persist in hiring men to play upon our college teams. As to such men one can only say that, if a cad comes into your company, you cannot very well escape the effects of his caddishness; but you can wish that you were free from his company.

§ 7

If it were not for repeated experiences to the contrary, it would hardly seem necessary to say that this paper is not intended as an attack upon college games. I do not think that college students play too many intercollegiate games. I do not think that they have too much interest in athletic sports. I. should like to see every student in a college playing some game and learning to play it well. And here it should in fairness be said that in some cases the income from intercollegiate games has been used wisely for the providing of fields and equipment for just such general enjoyment of athletic play. But, quite apart from this, I believe in the intercollegiate games of students both because of what they are and because of what they do for the communities which take part in them. Athletic sport is a fine and splendid thing in the life of any young man, of any community of young men. This paper is written in protest against the spoiling of that sport by using it for other purposes.

I believe in college education but I do not believe in furthering it by the abuse of the play of students. My observation is that when that attempt is made we spoil not only the play but also the education.

THE NEXT HUNDRED YEARS

CENTENNIAL EXERCISES, AMHERST, JUNE, 1921

THE NEXT HUNDRED YEARS

MY first words will seem, I fear, somewhat ungracious to you who come to listen to me. For I am planning to speak, not to you who are here but to others who are not here— persons who are far away, in time if not in space. And further, it must be said, this preference of hearers is dictated, in part at least, by the craving of a speaker for an audience which is interested, which will listen eagerly to what he has to say. "But surely," you will protest, "our presence here is proof enough of interest; why do you pass us by in favor of some other men who have not come?" And I must answer for my chosen hearers, "They would have liked to come but could not get away in time." And if you then demand to know who they may be and why, if so much interested, they could not come when others could, I will explain. There are two groups of them. Each would have had to travel a hundred years to be in time to-day. But even that, I am sure, they would gladly have done had time allowed. The men I have in mind are, first, those who discussed our theme one hundred years ago when Amherst was establishd and, second, those who, one hundred years from now, will talk upon the theme again when next we have centennial celebrations. Can you not see them there on either hand, the spokesmen of the founders, the spokesmen of the century after this? Would they not like to come to match their speech with ours? Would we not like to have them here? I wish they might appear in very person that we might really be acquainted with them. But failing that, I try to send my words across the years to them. And you may listen as I speak for you to them. And while we celebrate, on either side these friendly judges of our thought shall stand, two groups two hundred years apart, the spokesmen of the past, the spokesmen of the future.

I have a special personal reason for craving the presence here of Noah Webster and Aaron Leland and Zephaniah Swift Moore and Messrs. X and Y and Z of 2021. Facing to-day the task which those have faced one hundred years ago and these must face one hundred years from now, I feel their kinship and I give them mine. The founders had ideals. For the sake of these

they even tried to tear old Williams from the
rocky hills which held her fast.   And when they
could not break her bonds they tore a rib from out
her side and brought it here—I will not press the
figure further.   What were the fundamental
yearnings of the soul that drove them on to
violence such as this?   That was the question
which Webster, Leland, and Moore were called
upon to answer.   And Messrs. X, Y, Z must try
to state ideals, too.   A place without such things
is not a college.   And they, like us, will tumble
out in 2021 the dusty pages of the past, will look
to see what words were said two hundred years,
one hundred years before.   I doubt not we shall
have for them the same quaint, far-off quality
that Aaron, Noah, and Zephaniah have for us.
I doubt not they will smile when names and
phrases common to us strike oddly on their
modern ears.   And yet I know that they will
come to us and to our predecessors before they
state their modern purposes.   They dare not
frame a guiding purpose for the college which is
not in some fundamental sense our own.   Nor
may we in these earlier days so form our thought
that it shall not be true for them in differing
circumstance.   We speakers have a common
cause to serve, a single truth to follow through-

out these centuries. And so we stand together in a fellowship. Alike we shake and tremble before the awful task; with equal pain we know how little of the truth our words can tell; and hence, with friendly smile at one another, we put ourselves aside, and fix our eyes upon the common goal. Here, then, we talk together, centennial speakers. And you, who are in present human form the cause for which we speak, shall listen and judge. You shall judge us who try to say in words the truth by which you too are judged as well as we.

Such is the audience. What of the theme? It asks, "What does the college hope to be in this next century?" It is not strange that one should hesitate before a theme like this. I feel inclined to say to those who ask the question, "I'll answer you this if you'll answer another." Will some one kindly tell me just what some other things will be in this next century? What will the world be like, and what America, and what New England, and what our students, and what we? Do men say Peace or War, do they say Hope or Fear, do they say Beauty or Ugliness as they survey the coming years? What will that world be like for which we give our education? It makes a difference to our purposes. I cannot

tell you what Amherst hopes to be unless I know
what are the greater hopes of which ours are a
little part, to which our purposes must be con-
formed. One cannot talk of education unless one
knows the human spirit and its world. To teach
young people is to make them ready for the world
in which they are to live. Here is a constant task
which runs in changing form, through all the
centuries—the task of Webster, Moore, and
Leland, the task of X, Y, Z, our task as well. We
are and were and are to be a liberal college. But
in what world and for what spirits? Are they
the same as they have been before or do they
differ? According as they change so liberal
training changes; as they are constant, so liberal
teaching is the same. But will this coming century differ from the past or will it be the same?
Our theme requires that we should know what
things will be, will come to pass in this next century. It does not tell us where such information may be found.

So much for hearers and for theme! What of
the speaker's part? I am to tell you what I can
about the world and men, and hence of education,
in this next century—their constant meanings
and their changing forms. Over against the
thrilling story of the past I must attempt to

sketch the uncertain future. And as I give this prophecy I do not hope for your agreement, nor even for my own. Prophets, men say, are seldom honored near their homes. But may I ask you to take note that he who makes a prophecy is even nearer to his home than are his critics. To prophesy is not to know. Our prophecies are hopes and wills, desires and yearnings for the common weal in coming days. The prophet says, "Is not this good?" stating in words the values which we all accept. And when we answer "Yes," he says, "Then this must follow; this shall the future be." But round the corner some one else has drawn another vision from the same accepted truth. "No, no," he says, "the future shall be that." And while they clash, the sober unprophetic men, who do find honor near their homes—the nearer the home, the greater the honor—these shake their dubious heads and go to work again. That is their prophecy. And so, I say, I do not ask for your agreement. Prophets do not agree. I simply try to see and state my hopes of what a world may be, my pride in what a college might achieve. And you and you and you, out of our common cause, make different hopes and different expectations. By difference such as this we rightly plan together for a common end. But while we plan and differ as we may I still can count in special ways upon my special hearers, on Webster, Moore, and Leland, on X and Y and Z. They cheer me on to play the game. Those say, "We guessed and missed and hit—and so will you." And these, when their turn comes, will read the words and say, "Such was his guess, and theirs"; and then will take their turn and guess again.

But here to-day, they stand on either hand, my kinsmen. And we who speak for Amherst as she is will face with level eye the men that Amherst was, the men that Amherst is to be.

I

The prophecy which I am about to make falls into two parts, the first telling what the world is to be in the next century, the second deducing from this the future history of education. In each of these fields I have one and only one general observation to make. I shall try to make one prophecy about the world and then to derive from this one prophecy about the college. But under each of these two general principles you will find three minor principles, in each case the remarks on education being derived from the corresponding remarks upon the nature of the world.

You will note at once that in spite of the brave words of my introduction I am not planning to tell you all that will happen in the world in the next century. I am concerned simply with one feature of the world which is of special interest to a college, to this college. We must begin, therefore, by stripping our theme.

And first, since our location is now quite definitely fixed, we find in space a very obvious principle of limitation. We are American. We are not essentially of this town, nor of this State, nor even of New England. And only in rather scattered ways does our immediate influence go to other countries. We are primarily of this country and not of any part of it. This is an American college.

And, second, we are also a liberal college. As such our interest has to do only with central and essential things. We are concerned primarily with what men call, for lack of better terms, a country's culture. By this we mean that mingling of feeling, belief, purpose, expression, action, in which a nation's spirit finds itself revealed. A liberal college tries to learn and teach that culture.

What, then, in this next century, will be the culture of America? And in its making what part will be liberal colleges, this liberal college, play? This is the theme on which to-day we speakers speak together.

My general prophecy as to America has to do with National Independence. It is this. We, thus far, have been in cultural ways a dependent people. The time has come when we must win our independence. Thus far, I think it may be said, we have been busy giving to an old culture a new home. The home we have been making, and we have made it big. The culture we have received from others; we have not made it for ourselves. But now the time has come when we must win our freedom, must be ourselves, must master our spirit—when feelings, beliefs, and actions must be our own as they have never been before. We are, I think, in this next century destined to make a culture and to cease from merely taking one which others made.

May I explain by illustration. We have believed in freedom of individual life. Our fathers took this as a guiding principle. They found it in their blood; they took its formula from France and England. And we have kept it on our books and in our minds. But do we now

believe it when time of heavy pressure comes?
We are not sure.   Our action is uncertain.   And
why is this?   It does not mean that we are fickle
stock.   When once our will is fixed by clear,
deliberate choice, that choice will stand the strain
of bitter obstacles.   But as to freedom our will is
not yet fixed by clear, deliberate choice.   The
times have changed since first our fathers put the
word upon the books.   And we have never really
questioned whether with changing times freedom
itself should change.   We have the word which
others gave and yet we have not made it ours;
we do not know its present meaning.   Our home
we have made; we have not made our spirit.

If I may change the figure, I should say that
in cultural ways we have been playing school-boy
in face of older men, our teachers.   And while,
like school-boys, we have learned our lessons, we
have, like them, been growing up in strength and
power of body.   What I am saying does not
mean that we as individual men are children and
school-boys; it does not mean that leaders among
us are not wise and keen.   It does mean that we,
a people, have not yet willed what we shall be,
have not yet made our spirit by a choice which
understands itself.   No better illustration could
be found than what we did and failed to do in

the Great War. We went in mighty strength and
grew in strength by using it. We went with
courage and resolve, for we had found something
to do that seemed worth doing. We put our
purpose into words, clear-cut and ringing words
that stirred men's hearts. And now we are not
sure just what they were about. The victory is
won, and we are puzzled. And Europe smiles;
it cannot help but smile. We had such splendid
power, such eager spirit to play our part, and yet
we do not seem to have brought about just what
our spoken words had seemed to mean we were
determined should be brought about. And older
peoples look at us in envy of our youth and
strength, in admiration of our generous courage,
and yet in somewhat friendly, somewhat bitter
amusement at our futility. We did not understand the part we rushed to play.

But now the time has come for leaving school.
The baffled, awkward school-boy learns by sharp
experience such as we have had; he learns by
feeling of his strength at work. "They care
what I can do," he says, "but do they care for
my opinion? They like to have me on their side,
but do they really care what I may think about
the point at issue?" And then the questioning,
once begun, goes on. "What do I think; what

have I thought; who really has decided all these things that I have done, or tried to do, or thought that I was doing? It seems to me I 'd better look around and see just where I am.'' That time of questioning has come, I think, for us. In all the arts of peace as well as those of war we must put on the garments of a man. We can no longer merely learn what others have to teach. We must be independent, must be masters of our spirit, must make a culture of our own.

What will this independence mean for us? Many a boy mistakes the meaning of his manhood when it comes. And so may we. What does it mean?

It does not mean that we shall change our point of view, our values, or our standards, that we shall make a culture different from the one we had. Nor does it mean that we shall keep them as they were. It simply means that we shall choose whether or not to keep them as they were. When freedom comes a son may choose the way his father trod or, just as freely, he may choose some other way. The son who must discard his father in order to feel himself a man is still a boy; he has another choice to make when he becomes a man. The son who dare not tread a way his father has not smoothed and marked for him had better stay at home and keep his father on the watch for fear some bogy catch him.   And both these types of fear are now aroused among us as we approach our manhood.   Men fear that we shall leave the old, established ways, shall lose the spirit of Old New England, of Old Virginia, shall cease to think the thoughts our fathers made.   And others, just as timid in their braggadocio, fear we may keep the old, established ways, fear we may fail in being different from the past, fear lest the past may have the strength of youth still in its veins.   These fears of either type do not express our independence.   They are our tremblings at the brink, our first quick, timorous shrinkings from the facts which we must face.   They must be put aside as we go forward on our way.

And as men fear to be or not to be the past, so do they fear to be or not to be their neighbors. Our independence does not mean that we must take some foreign culture as our own.   Nor does it mean that we must hate all foreign cultures, that we must fashion for ourselves some mode of life of which no other race has ever dreamed.   But here again already men are raising frightened voices in angry warfare of conflicting views. "Shall foreign tastes and standards come across the seas to scoff at ours?" Or, on the other hand, "Shall we be mere provincials, rude, untutored folk who fail to eat and dress and talk and think as foreign peoples do?" These are the words of children aping at manhood. Freedom does not consist in likeness to other men nor yet in difference from them. Freedom is choice. And choice is Independence.

And so I dare to guess that in this coming century America will choose her way of life, will make a culture of her own. And when she does she will not act from fear or hate or prejudice or spite. Rather, in more objective ways, her fate will come upon her and she will see and take it gladly. One hundred million people here, linked by a common fate, must find, will find a way of life. And these first years of strong and youthful manhood will flush with glory of the new-found aims and new-found independence. These will be days in which to live. I know that often we shall trip and stumble. I know that very slowly will the nation as a whole be brought to tread a common way. And yet there is a way that we shall tread, a call that we shall answer. It calls us on from youth to manhood, from tutelage to self-direction, from strength to wis-

dom in the use of strength.   And we will answer
to the call.   Those who have known our youth
have little doubt of that.

But what will be the call?   What culture shall
we make?   There are three phases of our life,
our growth, concerning which I dare to guess our
choice.   The first concerns a racial aristocracy.
The second has to do with what we call Idealism.
The third deals with our Faith.

§ 1

And first I wish to speak of Anglo-Saxons and
of aristocracy.   We are in our beginnings the
sons of Britain.   Hers are our language, our literature, our law.   Hers is the culture from which
our culture springs.   In all essential things we
spring from Britain.

In still another more immediate sense we are
of British stock.   Her task is ours.   Britain has
gathered up the peoples of the earth and made
them one—one commonwealth or empire.   And
so have we.   To us they come from North and
South, from East and West, and we must make
them one—one single nation with a single life.
And as we face her task again we well may try to
learn what Britain has to teach, may look to see

what she has tried to do, where she has failed,
what ends she has achieved.

If we may separate England abroad from
England at home, I think that one may fairly say
that England's way of dealing with this task per-
force is one of Aristocracy. She governs other
races and yet she keeps herself apart; they are
not of her kind, her class. Peoples of many
creeds, of many colors, many grades of culture,
she holds together for some common ends. And
yet so far as foreign races are concerned, it is
not fellowship that welds the empire, but common
ends, external interests. And through it all,
Britain is leader; she stands above, apart.

What I have tried to say just now may be
attempted in another way. Britain has shown
the modern world how one people may take control of other peoples, may lead them in coöperation. In doing this Britain has faced the facts
—and so must we. For certain ends it was and
is desirable that races join together in external
ways, that they coöperate. Who should take
charge of this coöperation? They who in wisdom and in strength could do it best. And
Britain has rightly claimed her place. No other
nation in modern times has shown such wisdom
and such strength for just this task. And yet

for Britain it has ever been a task external to herself, an outside thing that needed to be done.

I press this externality because it marks so clearly the difference of the forms in which the common task appears. We, too, have many races, peoples, creeds, who must have government. But Britain's foreign peoples are, for the most part, outside her borders. Her subject races stretch around the globe, far from the little isle that sits so tight just off the coast of Western Europe. Our foreign peoples, on the other hand, are here within our borders; they are our neighbors, soon our fellow-citizens; our friends or not our friends; they are Americans. And so to Britain's son there comes again the task of Britain, but in a very different way.

And we must understand how different is the way. We cannot simply follow Britain's lead as if the situations were the same. Britain has many lands to govern. To each with her experienced eye she measures the closeness of the touch, the tightness of the bond. And so she has learned the lesson of taking charge of those who are not one's associates. That is Aristocracy. Is that the way for us? It cannot be. We have no power to choose how close shall be the touch, how tight the bonds that bind us all together.

Here we are, say what we will, a single people in a single land. If Britain's strains should prove too great she might again send off a separate people into independence. And neither of the two would suffer vital hurt. But we are one in many; we cannot, will not let a separate race, a separate part, a separate faction go. We may not separate. How shall we live together?

Here is, it seems to me, the urgent question for our Anglo-Saxon stock. Shall we again attempt an Anglo-Saxon aristocracy in this new world? Already in a sense it is established here without our will. We were the first to come; ours are the greater numbers still; ours are the language, literature, and law; we hold in greater part the places of influence and control; we have the education largely in our hands. We are predominant. And this has come not by our choice but by the mere blind play of fact. But now the time of choosing is at hand. Do we intend to make our dominance secure? Are we determined to exalt our culture, to make it sovereign over others, to keep them down, to have them in control? Or will we let our culture take its chance on equal terms, without advantage, taking its own in the free play of a great people's

fusing life? Which shall it be—an Anglo-Saxon
aristocracy of culture or a Democracy?

It is not easy for a stock like ours to make the
latter choice, and yet I think we will. We have
two sets of impulses at war within us. We have
a love of independence for ourselves; perhaps a
habit of ruling others. But there is still another
stronger side. I mean the willingness to take a
fair and honest chance, to play the game according to the rules and let the end be what it will.
And now the question is, which side will have its
way with us.

There are some obvious facts which might
direct our choice. We have already here one
people whom we rule, with whom we do not
genuinely associate. How many more such subject races would we like to have? And England
at home gives further evidence. Norman and
Saxon, Dane and Celt, have made a single people.
England did not fight Scotland down, nor did she
make much of it when she tried. But they have
fused together, and now are one. And who controls their common life, a Scotsman's modesty
forbids my saying. But just across the channel
is another people who have not fused, who fear
their culture may be lost, who dread and hate the

threat of domination. England and Ireland are not so happy as are the other pair.

Which shall it be with us? I hope that we shall ask no special favors for our thoughts, nor take such special favors as our power and influence might win were we to use them. Ours is the creed which says that every creed must take its chance with every other on equal footing. I hope that we shall value its being true more than we value its being ours. But many, I know, will bitterly object. "What will you have," they say; "shall we give up our culture; shall we desert beliefs and attitudes and purposes by which we live; shall we set these aside in favor of some sentimental common thing which men may all accept because no one of them accepts it?" "No, no," they say, "this truth is mine; it shall prevail if I have power to make it." And other men, whose truths are beaten down, are saying in their turn, "This is not fair; wait till I get my chance; and then we'll see whose truth shall win." And victories are won on fields like these, poor, silly, hollow, lying victories in which both sides are beaten. We do not want, we dare not have such victories in America.

And so I cast my Anglo-Saxon vote for Pure Democracy. We Anglo-Saxons have the upper

hand. How shall we use it? According to the
principles on which the country's life by us was
founded. We dare to say that even those principles must take their chance. He has deserted
them who will not let them face the test. Here
in America the peoples of the earth are working
out a common destiny in which each group must
share, share as it may according to the strength
and virtue that its spirit has. And we like all
the rest shall lose our separate life in this great
venture, shall lose it in trying to find, to make a
common life more fair, more free, more true than
men have ever seen before. It is a dangerous
game to play; but yet one dare not miss the
chance of playing it.

§ 2

My second guess as to our forming culture concerns Idealism. The term is not exact but it will
do.

To many who watch us from outside, America
presents a curious contrast in which again perhaps our sonship to the older Anglo-Saxon country is revealed. To quote a vulgar phrase, one
hears men say of us, "You seek the good, and get
the goods." They mean that we express ideals

and achieve success. And underneath the formula there lurks a query, "Which are you really? If one were seeking for your soul, should he dig down where words crop out or where the actions are? Which are you—devotees of Mammon or of Righteousness?"

It will not do to meet this question with too clear an answer. We are like other men; and other men, like us, are made of strangely mingled and conflicting elements. Men are of general stuff in special mixtures. What is with us the special kind of mixture?

Our fathers came across the sea with mingled motives. They sought a place of freedom and a means of livelihood. They wanted both, but in unusual degree they wanted freedom. And for the sake of this they risked the livelihood, took chances with it. And then the venture turned out well; from risky living fortune came; and then, great wealth. Such is our early history. And for the later immigrants the record is the same. They too have come in search of freedom and in hope of wealth. And here they have found a fertile continent ready to be their home, to give a lavish livelihood. But they have also found a people ready to risk its home, its wealth, if need be, for a cause. And sometimes need has come; and we have taken the risk; and it has turned out well; we have been fortunate. The Lucky Idealists, I think we may be called.

Such is the record of our youth. What will it be when school-boy days are past? The cynic tells of boys who dream great dreams when they are young, who love their fellows more than they love themselves. And cynics say of such a boy, "His father spoils him, lets him dream nonsense. Wait till his father stands aside, wait till he faces the cares that men must bear; those things will knock the nonsense out of his head." And cynics say the same of us. We have had lavish, easy, wealthy youth. And our Idealism, except in times of special crisis, has not had heavy strain to bear. What will become of it when easy youth is past, when we must face the cares of men? Will it go up like smoke, like idle dream? No, it will not. Youth is not always silly nor cynics always right. In easy youth, free from the pull of special interest, boys learn objective truth, and if they have in them the stuff of which a man is made, they do not turn their backs and run when danger comes. And we, in times of coming strain, will not desert our colors, but seeing the threat against them, will gather round them once again and risk our all for them again, and win again for them—and for ourselves, if we are fortunate.

But some one, future, past, or present, will ask, "What is this something which you call Idealism? What does it mean?" It has been put in many forms in many times and countries. With us it means something like this: Each man, each woman, each child shall have a chance at life; they shall not be denied the full and free and rich expression of themselves if we can help them to attain it. Men's lives are thwarted, stunted, twisted, throttled, killed by circumstance of every sort. That is our failure, even more than theirs. We will not have it so. Each life shall be what it might be, what may be made of it, what under favoring circumstances it may become. Such is our aim. What can we do? We cannot be the life, we cannot live for others in that sense. But we can shape the circumstance. That we will do. Wherever in the world we find men, women, children, weak in life, sickening in spirit because of circumstance that starves or beats them down, there we will fight the circumstance and break it. Wherever in the world the sun shines on the human spirit, there we will take our friends that they may bask and grow and be themselves. Lives shall be made successful; each one shall have as good a chance at being itself as we can make this hard old world provide. We are responsible. That is, it seems to me, Idealism as we have seen it.

How shall we see it in the coming century as we go out from youth to manhood? Simply with better understanding, as befits a man. Thus far our thoughts are chiefly negative. We have said, "All men are equal in our eyes; all men have equal rights before the laws which limit them; no man shall interfere with others; this is the land of opportunity." That is the creed as boys perceive it. But now we need a version for a man. There is not one among us whose thought and action do not take him far beyond this point. "People must have an equal chance," we say. But, more than that, each one must have some chance of taking the chances which he has. We know that rich men's sons often have little chance of taking what life presents them; they are too dulled by lavish circumstance. And we resent the horror of it. So too with others. If children cannot walk, little is gained by them from public running tracks; if children do not feel what reading is, they are not helped by libraries; if children live in degradation until their souls are stupefied, one does not say much when one talks of opportunity. What does it mean to give to men a chance? Is it to stand aside; is it to say that they are free to roam when all men know that chains have bound them fast? No, it is more than that. It means that men shall not be bound by chains, whether their own or forged by other men. It means that every man shall have a genuine chance at taking the ways of life that lie before him. It means that life shall be; that men shall really live; life shall not be denied. We take responsibility.

And so I think that in the coming century, Idealism will mean, not simply letting others be themselves, but acting that each shall be himself. I am not speaking here for any special scheme of social betterment. I do not know what can be done by way of helping older people. The Puritan believes two doctrines at this point, first that his duty is to help his fellow-men, and second, that to help another man destroys his character —and that is sin. Between two sins like these, one's action lags. And I am much a Puritan. But Puritan or not, I know one field in which Idealism may have its way without the fear of sin. Young people may be, must be helped to grow into their strength. Young lives shall not be stunted and deformed. In youth we have the human being in our hands to make it ready for its life, ready in every phase and aspect of its being. This is the time for making sure that lives succeed, by care and nurture as they grow; all children, every child must be so trained and disciplined, so nourished and protected, so strengthened and refined, so guided and informed that richness of life shall open up before it and it shall see and take what life affords. This is the task of Education in the broader sense. In face of it our present schemes of schools and training are petty, trivial things. No other task which men attempt compares with it in grandeur or in scope. Here in the care of youth, in this next century, American Idealism will find its richest play.

§ 3

My last prophecy as to America's culture in this next century has to do with Faith. A century ago, when Amherst was established, men spoke much of their faith. To-day men on the whole speak little of it. What they will do one hundred years from now, who knows? And yet the change, whatever it may be, is not essential. Men do not really change in things so deep as this. What is that constant Faith which men have had or failed to have, which they will have or fail to have in this next century?

My friends who study our national life tell me that a century ago America was much as she is now. The world had been at war in long and bitter conflict. And we had had our share of it. And there had come upon the people the degradation which follows after struggle. Fiber had slackened; standards were broken down; customs were insecure; men seemed to have lost their grip upon the world and on themselves. Against this degradation leaders of men were lashing out with eager words. Among the cries there rose the words of those who founded Amherst College. They saw and felt the need of strength and virtue in the common life. They called for men to bring them back again. And chiefly in their time they called for ministers to preach. "A Plea for a Miserable World"—that was the sermon delivered by Daniel Clark when the building of the Charity Institution was begun in August, 1820. It was the call of Noah Webster who, on the same occasion, summoned men out from the "barbarous works of war" into the establishment of the "empire of truth." To these men and to their fellows it seemed that the wisdom of this world had turned to folly and to shame.

Over against it they preached another wisdom by which the loss might be regained.

No man among us, I suppose, would use to-day the words and phrases which were used one hundred years ago. Nor do we think the thoughts in just the forms which then seemed true. And yet the essential cleavage which they knew is with us still. There are two ways of facing life, two kinds of wisdom for mankind. One is the way of dread, the other the way of confidence. One rests on fear and cunning; the other on hope and faith. One is for man, the beast; the other, for man the spirit.

And as between these two, the issue is a very simple one, no matter what the terms in which it may be put. The question is, Do we rely upon the world to be with men as they pursue the good? Is good supported and sustained outside ourselves, or do we fight alone in desperate single-handedness? That is the ancient modern query that cuts in two our ways of life, that cuts each man in two, that cuts the groups of men apart.

And by men's actions are they judged in this respect. The men who fight for justice, as they say, and yet who fight unjustly, do not believe in justice. They dare not let it have its way, care for itself. They think themselves and their injustice greater in power to serve its ends than justice is. The men who fight for truth with lies strike at the very heart of truth. One sees men fighting, as they think, upon the side of God, who fight as if the world were ruled by devils. They fear, resort to subterfuge, seek favor, give way to hate, and so despair that every breath they draw denies the faith for which they fight. They have not genuine faith; they live in cautious fear.

This lack of faith appears to-day most clearly in our cleverness. We have become too shrewd in recent years. We trust too much in management, in propaganda, in administration. We moderns threaten to become past masters in the art of telling truthful lies, of doing deeds of justice by which our pockets shall be filled. We know too well the tricks of using for our ends both men and truth. We know just what to say and when, to whom and in what form. And every one to whom we speak must ask, "Who pays to have that said; why does he say just that; what is he holding back?" We do not trust our world; and hence we dare not trust each other. But what we need to learn again is what the faithful men have known through all the centuries. The truth suppressed will out; truth cannot be denied. And he whose pockets overflow with money gained by craft is poorer for the having. An end achieved by guile is lost. This world is such that craft and guile are bad; it has no love for folly, and yet it loves an honest fool more than a clever knave. Such faith as this we need again to save us from our trust in cleverness.

Shall we regain our faith in this next century? I hope we shall; I think we will. Just now we are bewildered by the many novel things with which we have to deal. Change after change has come so fast that we have lost our bearings. We have not made a code to fit the changing scheme; we still are lost within a whirl that leaves us dizzy as it rushes past. But we shall find our bearings, shall get our grip anew upon the world. And we will fashion principles which need not be denied when put in practice. The world is such that we have right to faith. And as a hundred years ago, men claimed that right and sought again their faith, so now we will again make good our claim. Without it life is for most of us a hollow mockery. We are too fond of life to let it go like that. America, I think, will live again by faith.

II

Such is my prophecy about the world, about America, in the next century. If it were true, what would it mean for education, for liberal education, for education here in Amherst?

I have said that in this next century America will pass from youth to manhood, will try to make a culture of its own. And further, out of the mingling of the peoples of the earth, a greater people will be fashioned here. And we will care for individual human beings, will make the individual lives of men the ends we serve. And we will serve these ends without denying them, will keep the faith that they have rightness in themselves. If such should be the process of our country's life, what will it mean for liberal colleges; what will it mean for us? The college is a place where men and boys are sensitive to human life, are set apart to share by vision and by understanding in the world of men. What will the vision be in this next century? How shall we understand? Let us attempt to answer point by point according to the prophecy.

And first, the major prophecy. If we, the country, go from youth to manhood, so will the college. It, too, has been thus far a formless place of vagueness and of irresponsibility. America has dallied at the door of manhood, and so have we. Our colleges have failed for lack of conscious purpose in their teaching. And young Americans are hard to teach because neither to them nor to their friends has come the sense of tasks that must be done. Our talk of personal opportunity is far too pale, too negative a thing to claim the generous and adventurous mind. And so those minds are taken, not by us, but by a hundred petty, trivial things, each for its passing moment. But now the time has come when we must claim those minds as ours, to serve our purposes and theirs. I do not mean that we must find sham causes to allure our youth, invent high purposes to tempt them on to lessons, like donkeys straining for a tuft of fragrant grass. But this I mean. If we have purposes to serve, if we have manhood's obligations to fulfil, the college, first of all, must catch the sense of what they are. Here boys and men must feel and know and share their people's life. Here, if our people strive, the sense of striving must be strong and deep. Here, if our people fail, whether in virtue or in skill, the sense of shame

must sting and throb until the failure is re-
deemed. Here, if we win, the joy of winning
must explode in riotous delight. Here, as our
people seek to find their way, we must be seeking, too, and help to find the way.

Our people go to find their destiny. What will
the college do? It, too, will go to find its fate with
free and honest purpose. There will be many days
of doubt and danger, of strain and sad confusion.
But through it all we shall go out as boys from
their commencement, from eager youth to eager,
sober manhood. This is the time when purpose
forms because great things are seen. Life will
have zest and power. There are no days in life
like those in which the man breaks out into himself. And boys, whose strongest craving is to be
like men, will rush to share that zest. Amherst
and Williams, Harvard and Yale will live again,
as in the earlier days when they were first established, to be the nervous centers of a growing life.
It will be good to try to see and tell the way our
people ought to choose to go.

What will the college be in this next century?
Out of the nation's life its purposes will come.
What will they be? I have three minor prophe-
cies to make.

§ 1

First, if we are not to have a racial aristocracy, democracy must have a dwelling-place within our colleges. If here, where thought is free and men are young, we dare not let our Anglo-Saxon culture take its chance, no other men or institutions will take the risk. We are an Anglo-Saxon college; and so in greater part we must remain. And yet we are American. We may not keep ourselves apart either from persons or from cultures not our own. We dare not shut our gates to fellow-citizens nor to their influence. So we must welcome boys of other stocks. And if they do not come, we must go out and bring them in. Our undergraduate life must represent the country which it serves; students must keep it free from any taint of caste or aristocracy. And teachers, too, must keep our teaching free, open to all the riches which our people have to bring. We shall not lose our Shakspere by learning Dante's world; nor is one false to Poe because one follows Dostoyevsky. Our mother England gave us much; and yet she has not all that men may have. Peoples who rule tend to know more of ruling life than living it. And we, our mother's very

eager sons, are much excited by the rattle of machinery. We need the wealth of spirit which the
other peoples have to give. And they need us.
Here in the American college that fusion must be
made, our people must be formed and shaped into
the rounded wholeness of a single life. This is
a splendid college task. We are and must be
genuinely American.

§ 2

And, second, if in this coming century our people are to care for individual lives, the college
has a heavy part to play. The college is the top-
most round of general education. Here taste for
what is best must find its best expression. Here
wisdom must be found as nowhere else, wisdom
about the ways and means of making lives successful. But more specifically there is an urgent
task which colleges have much neglected in the
past. We must have conscious part in general
national education. I do not know whether or not
within one hundred years the state will take us as
her own. I dare not prophesy on matters such as
that. But I do know that in all genuine
meanings of the term we are a people's college,
and shall continue so to be. And we must share

more deeply in the broader work of making younger people ready for their living. The Greeks have said how hard it is for a democracy to keep in touch with excellence. And popular education, popular training of our youth tends ever downward in a democratic people's life. Shall we have shoddy training for our youth? We have it now in large degree. And out of shoddy training shoddy people come. But as, of old, men called for ministers to preach and lead, so we to-day must call for ministers and teachers of every sort who shall take charge of education, shall give it excellence from which to draw its strength. To bring the best we have of taste and insight into the making of our youth—that is a splendid task which liberal colleges must face. I do not mean that colleges should be made normal schools for teachers; I do not mean that we should cease from sending graduates to law, to business, to medicine, to all the various arts of human life. But I do mean that in some deeper sense our colleges which have in charge the best that human life affords must make the best effective in the care of all our youth.

We must send forth more ministers and teachers. And we must make them ready for their work. We cannot cultivate our youth unless their teachers have themselves been cultivated in taste and insight. Here is the essential weakness of our national scheme of teaching. It is not based on genuine education of those who do the teaching. Only an educated people can, in the last resort, give education to its children. And we are vainly trying to pay for education rather than to give it. But we, the colleges, must set the standard high, must make it gleam before the people's eyes, must lead them into the love of truth, into the search for wisdom in the ways of life. For this was Amherst College founded; by this it is and must be justified.

§ 3

And lastly, what of faith? Our country seeks to find its bearings, to get a grip again upon some fundamental things in which it may have confidence. What will the college do to help? It must keep faith itself. Life is secure. Beneath the strife of men there are the common things for which both parties, with their partial wisdom, partial blindness, strive. The college must keep in closer touch with these than with the parties which by different ways are striving toward them. Amid their doubts and differences men need to-day the sense of their agreements lying deep within themselves and in their world. Serenity and humor, good will and confidence, these are the qualities which colleges must keep in charge to serve their people. Men lose their poise in days like these, grow frightened by events which they themselves cannot control, take desperate means to save the situation by a single stroke; are willing just this once to put their faith aside, to save it for all future time. And colleges must tell them, what the ages have to tell, that single strokes do not save worlds, except for single moments. And if the faith is sacrificed to-day, it will cost more to win it back to-morrow. Here is, it seems to me, the deepest task of liberal colleges—to put the parties in their proper place and keep them there. We must have parties, and yet we need to smile at parties—I do not mean to laugh at them. We need to see each partial good as good in part, and yet as just a part. We need to smile and keep our faith in men and in their world. With all its doubts and fears, with all its conflict and confusion, the world of men moves onward toward its goal. And they who doubt the goal are doubting toward it; and they who find it here will some day learn that there as well it has been found by other men. It leads us on whether we will or not. It does not fear our doubts; nor does it value quite as highly as we sometimes do our approbations. It is the faith of men in Man and in the world. The colleges must keep, will keep that faith in this next century.

III

And now, one closing word! I know that some of you who listen to our conversation have said, "All this is very general, very remote, not very helpful for the special tasks which wait the college in these coming years." You ask, "What is to be the course of study; what will you teach and how? Is wisdom gained from Greek or science, art or statistics? Are we to have a junior-senior college plan? Shall senior majors live or be forgotten?"

And here again, I cannot tell you what will come to pass. Nor do I care to try. These things, important as they are, are not essential. They must be passed upon as current questions according as the spirit leads. Two things I know concerning them. First, we will keep in mind the stipulations made by Zephaniah Moore when he accepted office as president of Amherst College. He required assurance, first, that "the classical education should be thorough," and second, that "the course of study should not be inferior to that in the colleges of New England." In both these ways the college pledged itself to him; and it has tried to keep, will try to keep, that pledge. But further I am sure of one thing else. The course of study and the ways of teaching must be determined by the teachers, must be for them expressions of themselves. Nothing is gained by imposition from without. Trustees and president and graduates may make their plans, but they will fail unless they are as well the plans of those who do the teaching. Here is a truth which we must never lose from mind. Nine years ago I said, in an inaugural address, and now I say again, "It is, I believe, the function of the teacher to stand before his pupils and before the community at large as the intellectual leader of his time. If he is not able to take that leadership, he is not worthy of his calling. If the leadership is taken from him and given to others, then the very foundations of the scheme of instruction are shaken." We shall not lose these principles in these next years. A great college with great teachers, that is our dream for Amherst. A great college is great teachers

—that is the principle by which our dream comes true.

And so I say to Amherst men of every century, "We have a right to-day to faith in this old college, faith in the country which the college serves, faith in the work the college has to do, faith in its willingness and power to do that work. And we must keep the faith and do the work with joy and exultation." Listen, you men of Amherst's present day, listen and you will hear the cheers that come to urge us on. They come from out of the past, one hundred years ago; they ring from out the future, from centuries still to come. They are the cries of those who, after searching, try to speak the spirit of Amherst College. Listen to Webster, Moore, and Leland; listen to X and Y and Z. They shout from out the years to us, their fellows, "The college lives; long live the college!"

THE MACHINE CITY

Two Hundred and Fiftieth Anniversary of Founding of
Pawtucket, Rhode Island

THE MACHINE CITY

I AM asked to speak to you to-night on the future of this city. I know only one thing certain about its future, namely, that no one can tell what it will be.

This is, in an extreme degree, a machine city. I do not refer, Mr. Mayor, to the nature of its politics, but to the source of its power, the nature of its social forces. This city has been made by machines. Here Jencks set up his forge, here Slater began the manufacture of cotton. And since their day this group of people has led the way in the building and using of machines for the making of goods which men desire. We are a machine city. It is our strength, our glory—and our problem.

If one could tell the future of such a city as this, one could answer many urgent questions concerning the modern world at large. Modern civilization, especially in our Anglo-Saxon section of it, has likewise been made by machines. We have become an industrial people. What is to be

145

the future of an industrial civilization is a problem which vexes and tortures the spirit of any man who honestly and intelligently studies it. I should like to-night, on this occasion of our celebration of two hundred and fifty years of great achievement, to ask you to look with me at some of the implications which this achievement carries with it.

Machines have brought to men results, some of them aimed at, some of them quite unintended and unnoticed. May I give a very partial and hurried list of them?

First, machines have increased the numbers of our population and, at the same time, the supply of material wealth for the use of the population. The machine magnifies human work, makes it more efficient, multiplies it, in its effect, by ten, by a hundred, by a thousand it may be. It needs more people for its work; it can support more people by its products. As a result of the machine mode of life, we have more people in our communities, more wealth at their service.

But again, the machines have claimed the people themselves as parts of the machinery. They have made human life more mechanical. The machine which extends the power of the human body at the same time makes that body a part of itself. Men and women are taken into mills and shops and offices to be used, more than they were before, as tools, as instruments, as parts of a machine technique. The human life which uses machines is, in turn, used by them.

Again, machines have broken down the continuity and stability of towns and cities. They have changed the town from a settled group of individuals and families into a place through which people flow in constantly changing streams. The machines of transportation carry people off to other places in search of wealth and opportunity, while, on the other hand, the machines in the mills are ceaselessly dragging other peoples in from the ends of the earth to take their places in the mills. Our communities are no longer places of settled abode. They are changing, flowing streams made up of elements novel and strange and foreign each to the other, and ever replaced by others strange to them.

And still again, the machine has cut the family into parts, has broken down its continuity. Parents and children separate and go their different ways, do different work, think different thoughts, choose different friends; they scatter and separate, live unrelated lives far more than families have done before.

And through all this one other change has run in varying forms. While individual men have wandered and scattered, the net which holds them all has drawn more tightly in. The world is bound together in certain external, mechanical ways. We saw this in the recent war. That was no war of groups or tribes or even nations. It was the world at war, two huge, enormous forces fighting for mastery of our industrial power with every ounce of strength the world and its machines could give, being used to turn the scale. It was a war so great that all men had and all they were seemed to depend upon the issue, so great that many of us lived in ghastly fear that human life as we now have it would smash and go to pieces. Machines brought on the struggle, and when it came they made it monstrous in its power.

In these and other ways machines have changed our life under our very hands. But, now, what of the future? What will they make of us in days to come?

No man can tell what they will do to us. But we can tell what we will do to them. We will not let them use us as their tools. We will use them as tools of ours.

Mr. Mayor, I have a suggestion to make to you.

It is that this city which has taken the lead in the development of the machine industry of this country shall now take the lead in making sure that that industry contributes properly to the life of the people whom it pretends to serve. We must understand our machines if we are to use them, must find out what they are for, whether or not they serve the purposes for which we made them, whether they are bringing about evil results which we had not intended. We must understand these machines and their consequences if we would use them properly.

I would ask, Mr. Mayor, that you select a commission of twenty-five or thirty of your best men to study human living in an industrial town. There are three essential questions about human life: (1) what ought it to be, what is its proper form: (2) what things further, what things prevent its being as it ought to be: (3) what measures can we take to make it right, to smash aside the things that make it wrong? Those questions this city should study. What of the people in the mills, the shops, the offices, the banks, the homes, the schools? What of men and women and children? Are they as fine and right and happy as human beings ought to be? If not, why not? And what can be done to make them better?

Mr. Mayor, if our industrial civilization does not begin to understand itself and its machines, it must of course go down in ruins. The forces which it makes and finds are far too great to be let loose to run amuck without our human guidance. We must take them in hand by understanding them, by knowing ourselves and them, by making them our servants. If you, my friends, in this strong city will seek for wisdom to match your strength, you will be taking the lead in what the modern world must do if it would keep itself a proper abode for men, for women, for children. I ask you, Mr. Mayor, to take the lead in seeing that studying such as this is done.

There are one or two explanations which I should like to add to this proposal.

I am not advocating any theory as to men and their machines. I am not pleading for Socialism or Radicalism, for Conservatism or Americanism. I am pleading for honest study by honest men, of human living. Study is not for scholars only, not for colleges and universities alone. Study is an attempt at intelligence in dealing with human life. Study is the activity of a man who has something to do and who wishes to do it well. When studying is needed, they who neglect it are not simply failing to be scholars;

they are failing to be men; they fail where a man should be ashamed to fail without a desperate struggle.

And again, though it be somewhat ungracious, may I remind you that Rhode Island, industrial Rhode Island, seems to have special reason for self-examination. If one may take as they appear statistics from the surgeon-general in Washington, Rhode Island more than any other State failed in supply of proper men when men were needed for the army. For each one thousand men, the army found among you here a greater number of "defects," a greater number of defective men, a greater number of men unfitted for its service than any other State supplied. The facts suggest at least occasion for our study.

But finally, a word that bears more closely on my theme. You ask me of Pawtucket's future. What of its children then? They are its future. What do you make of them? I said just now I had no program of reform. But at this point I have a program. We are not taking proper care of children in this industrial life of ours. Wealth pours itself into our hands, and we are spending it in every way except in that which really counts —the making of children's lives as strong and fine and right as they might be. What we may do for them determines what our future is to be. If I were here among you as of old and serving again upon the School Board, I would ask the people of the city to multiply the school appropriation by ten; and then if that were not enough, to multiply again for taking proper care of children.

But, Mr. Mayor, I do not wish to interfere or dogmatize. I am not here to blame or criticize. Rather I glory in the strength and cleverness that have built up this place of industry. But now I ask for wisdom, too. I beg of you that here as elsewhere men make sure they have their living under their control. I ask that you, the men who make machines and make them run, shall try to know what they are running for, shall make them serve their proper ends, shall make them serve the children, the women, the men, whose instruments they are. Make human living right in this old town. To make it right you must attempt to understand it. Pawtucket's future would be a glorious one if it could lead the way in such an enterprise as that.

THE THEORY OF THE LIBERAL COLLEGE

INAUGURAL ADDRESS AS PRESIDENT OF AMHERST COLLEGE,
OCTOBER 16, 1912

THE THEORY OF THE LIBERAL COLLEGE [1]

IN the discussions concerning college education there is one voice which is all too seldom raised and all too often disregarded. It is the voice of the teacher and the scholar, of the member of the college faculty. It is my purpose here to consider the ideals of the teacher, of the problems of instruction as they present themselves to the men who are giving instruction. And I do this not because I believe that just now the teachers are wiser than others who are dealing with the same questions, but rather as an expression of a definite conviction with regard to the place of the teacher in our educational scheme. It is, I believe, the function of the teacher to stand before his pupils and before the community at large as the intellectual leader of his time. If he is

1 This address has previously appeared in a collection of papers, published in 1920 by the Marshall Jones Company of Boston, under the title, "The Liberal College." It has also been included in a number of collections of readings for college students in connection with courses in English.

not able to take this leadership, he is not worthy of his calling. If the leadership is taken from him and given to others, then the very foundations of the scheme of instruction are shaken. He who in matters of teaching must be led by others is not the one to lead the imitative undergraduate, not the one to inspire the confidence and loyalty and discipleship on which all true teaching depends. If there are others who can do these things better than the college teacher of to-day, then we must bring them within the college walls. But if the teacher is to be deemed worthy of his task, then he must be recognized as the teacher of us all, and we must listen to his words as he speaks of the matters intrusted to his charge.

In the consideration of the educational creed of the teacher I will try to give, first, a brief statement of his belief; second, a defense of it against other views of the function of the college; third, an interpretation of its meaning and significance; fourth, a criticism of what seem to me misunderstandings of their own meaning prevalent among the teachers of our day; and finally, a suggestion of certain changes in policy which must follow if the belief of the teacher is clearly understood and applied in our educational procedure.

§ 1

First, then, What do our teachers believe to be the aim of college instruction? Wherever their opinions and convictions find expression there is one contention which is always in the foreground, namely, that to be liberal a college must be essentially intellectual. It is a place, the teachers tell us, in which a boy, forgetting all things else, may set forth on the enterprise of learning. It is a time when a young man may come to awareness of the thinking of his people, may perceive what knowledge is and has been and is to be. Whatever light-hearted undergraduates may say, whatever the opinions of solicitous parents, of ambitious friends, of employers in search of workmen, of leaders in church or state or business—whatever may be the beliefs and desires and demands of outsiders—the teacher within the college, knowing his mission as no one else can know it, proclaims that mission to be the leading of his pupil into the life intellectual. The college is primarily not a place of the body, nor of the feelings, nor even of the will; it is, first of all, a place of the mind.

§ 2

Against this intellectual interpretation of the college our teachers find two sets of hostile forces constantly at work. Outside the walls there are the practical demands of a busy commercial and social scheme; within the college there are the trivial and sentimental and irrational misunderstandings of its own friends. Upon each of these our college teachers are wont to descend as Samson upon the Philistines, and when they have had their will, there is little left for another to accomplish.

As against the immediate practical demands from without, the issue is clear and decisive. College teachers know that the world must have trained workmen, skilled operatives, clever buyers and sellers, efficient directors, resourceful manufacturers, able lawyers, ministers, physicians and teachers. But it is equally true that in order to do its own work, the liberal college must leave the special and technical training for these trades and professions to be done in other schools and by other methods. In a word, the liberal college does not pretend to give all the kinds of teaching which a young man of college age may profitably receive; it does not even claim to give all the kinds of intellectual training which are worth giving. It is committed to intellectual training of the liberal type, whatever that may mean, and to that mission it must be faithful. One may safely say, then, on behalf of our college teachers, that their instruction is intended to be radically different from that given in the technical school or even in the professional school. Both these institutions are practical in a sense which the college, as an intellectual institution, is not. In the technical school the pupil is taught how to do some one of the mechanical operations which contribute to human welfare. He is trained to print, to weave, to farm, to build; and for the most part he is trained to do these things by practice rather than by theory. His possession when he leaves the school is not a stock of ideas, of scientific principles, but a measure of skill, a collection of rules of thumb. His primary function as a tradesman is not to understand but to do, and in doing what is needed he is following directions which have first been thought out by others and are now practised by him. The technical school intends to furnish training

which, in the sense in which we use the term, is
not intellectual but practical.

In a corresponding way the work of the professional school differs from that of the liberal
college. In the teaching of engineering, medicine, or law we are or may be beyond the realm
of mere skill and within the realm of ideas and
principles. But the selection and the relating of
these ideas is dominated by an immediate practical interest which cuts them off from the intellectual point of view of the scholar. If an undergraduate should take away from his studies
of chemistry, biology and psychology only those
parts which have immediate practical application
in the field of medicine, the college teachers
would feel that they had failed to give the boy
the kind of instruction demanded of a college.
It is not their purpose to furnish applied knowledge in this sense. They are not willing to cut
up their sciences into segments and to allow the
student to select those segments which may be of
service in the practice of an art or a profession.
In one way or another the teacher feels a kinship with the scientist and the scholar which forbids him to submit to this domination of his
instruction by the demands of an immediate practical interest. Whatever it may mean, he intends

to hold the intellectual point of view and to keep his students with him if he can. In response, then, to demands for technical and professional training our college teachers tell us that such training may be obtained in other schools; it is not to be had in a college of liberal culture.

In the conflict with the forces within the college our teachers find themselves fighting essentially the same battle as against the foes without. In a hundred different ways the friends of the college, students, graduates, trustees and even colleagues, seem to them so to misunderstand its mission as to minimize or to falsify its intellectual ideals. The college is a good place for making friends; it gives excellent experience in getting on with men; it has exceptional advantages as an athletic club; it is a relatively safe place for a boy when he first leaves home; on the whole it may improve a student's manners; it gives acquaintance with lofty ideals of character, preaches the doctrine of social service, exalts the virtues and duties of citizenship. All these conceptions seem to the teacher to hide or to obscure the fact that the college is fundamentally a place of the mind, a time for thinking, an opportunity for knowing. And perhaps in proportion to their own loftiness of purpose and motive

they are the more dangerous as tending all the
more powerfully to replace or to nullify the underlying principle upon which they all depend.
Here again when misconception clears away, one
can have no doubt that the battle of the teacher
is a righteous one. It is well that a boy should
have four good years of athletic sport, playing
his own games and watching the games of his fellows; it is well that his manners should be improved; it is worth while to make good friends;
it is very desirable to develop the power of understanding and working with other men; it is surely
good to grow in strength and purity of character, in devotion to the interests of society, in
readiness to meet the obligations and opportunities of citizenship. If any one of these be lack-
ing from the fruits of a college course we may
well complain of the harvest. And yet is it not
true that by sheer pressure of these, by the driving and pulling of the social forces within and
without the college, the mind of the student is
constantly torn from its chief concern? Do not
our social and practical interests distract our
boys from the intellectual achievements which
should dominate their imagination and command
their zeal? I believe that one may take it as the
deliberate judgment of the teachers of our col-

leges to-day that the function of the college is
constantly misunderstood, and that it is subjected
to demands which, however friendly in intent, are
yet destructive of its intellectual efficiency and
success.

§ 3

But now that the contention of the teacher has
been stated and reaffirmed against objections, it
is time to ask, What does it mean?   And how can
it be justified?   By what right does a company
of scholars invite young men to spend with them
four years of discipleship?   Do they, in their in-
sistence upon the intellectual quality of their
ideal intend to give an education which is avowedly unpractical?   If so, how shall they justify
their invitation, which may perhaps divert young
men from other interests and other companion-
ships which are valuable to themselves and to
their fellows?   In a word, what is the underlying
motive of the teacher, what is there in the intellectual interests and activities which seems to
him to warrant their domination over the training and instruction of young men during the college years?

It is no fair answer to this question to summon
us to faith in intellectual ideals, to demand of

us that we live the life of the mind with confidence in the virtues of intelligence, that we love knowledge and because of our passion follow after it. Most of us are already eager to accept intellectual ideals, but our very devotion to them forbids that we accept them blindly. I have often been struck by the inner contradictoriness of the demand that we have faith in intelligence. It seems to mean, as it is so commonly made to mean, that we must unintelligently follow intelligence, that we must ignorantly pursue knowledge, that we must question everything except the business of asking questions, that we think about everything except the use of thinking itself. As Mr. F. H. Bradley would say, the dictum, "Have faith in intelligence," is so true that it constantly threatens to become false. Our very conviction of its truth compels us to scrutinize and test it to the end.

How then shall we justify the faith of the teacher? What reason can we give for our exaltation of intellectual training and activity? To this question two answers are possible. First, knowledge and thinking are good in themselves. Secondly, they help us in the attainment of other values in life which without them would be impossible. Both these answers may be given and

are given by college teachers. Within them must
be found whatever can be said by way of explanation and justification of the work of the liberal
college.

The first answer receives just now far less of
recognition than it can rightly claim. When the
man of the world is told that a boy is to be
trained in thinking just because of the joys and
satisfactions of thinking itself, just in order that
he may go on thinking as long as he lives, the
man of the world has been heard to scoff and to
ridicule the idle dreaming of scholarly men. But
if thinking is not a good thing in itself, if intellectual activity is not worth while for its own
sake, will the man of the world tell us what is?
There are those among us who find so much satisfaction in the countless trivial and vulgar amuse-
ments of a crude people that they have no time
for the joys of the mind. There are those who
are so closely shut up within a little round of
petty pleasures that they have never dreamed of
the fun of reading and conversing and investi-
gating and reflecting. And of these one can only
say that the difference is one of taste, and that
their tastes seem to be relatively dull and stupid.
Surely it is one function of the liberal college to
save boys from that stupidity, to give them an

appetite for the pleasures of thinking, to make them sensitive to the joys of appreciation and understanding, to show them how sweet and captivating and wholesome are the games of the mind. At the time when the play element is still dominant it is worth while to acquaint boys with the sport of facing and solving problems. Apart from some of the experiences of friendship and sympathy I doubt if there are any human interests so permanently satisfying, so fine and splendid in themselves as are those of intellectual activity. To give our boys that zest, that delight in things intellectual, to give them an appreciation of a kind of life which is well worth living, to make them men of intellectual culture—that certainly is one part of the work of any liberal college.

On the other hand, the creation of culture as so defined can never constitute the full achievement of the college. It is essential to awaken the impulses of inquiry, of experiment, of investigation, of reflection, the instinctive cravings of the mind. But no liberal college can be content with this. The impulse to thinking must be questioned and rationalized as must every other instinctive response. It is well to think, but what shall we think about? Are there any lines

of investigation and reflection more valuable than
others, and if so, how is their value to be tested?
Or again, if the impulse for thinking comes into
conflict with other desires and cravings, how is
the opposition to be solved? It has sometimes
been suggested that our man of intellectual culture may be found like Nero fiddling with words
while all the world about him is aflame. And the
point of the suggestion is not that fiddling is a
bad and worthless pastime, but rather that it is
inopportune on such an occasion, that the man
who does it is out of touch with his situation,
that his fiddling does not fit his facts. In a word,
men know with regard to thinking, as with regard to every other content of human experience,
that it cannot be valued merely in terms of itself.
It must be measured in terms of its relation to
other contents and to human experience as a
whole. Thinking is good in itself—but what does
it cost of other things, what does it bring of
other values? Place it amid all the varied contents of our individual and social experience,
measure it in terms of what it implies, fix it by
means of its relations, and then you will know its
worth not simply in itself but in that deeper
sense which comes when human desires are rationalized and human lives are known in their

entirety, as well as they can be known by those who are engaged in living them.

In this consideration we find the second answer of the teacher to the demand for justification of the work of the college. Knowledge is good, he tells us, not only in itself, but in its enrichment and enhancement of the other values of our experience. In the deepest and fullest sense of the words, knowledge pays. This statement rests upon the classification of human actions into two groups, those of the instinctive type and those of the intellectual type. By far the greater part of our human acts are carried on without any clear idea of what we are going to do or how are we going to do it. For the most part our responses to our situations are the immediate responses of feeling, of perception, of custom, of tradition. But slowly and painfully, as the mind has developed, action after action has been translated from the feeling to the ideational type; in wider and wider fields men have become aware of their own modes of action, more and more they have come to understanding, to knowledge of themselves and of their needs. And the principle underlying all our educational procedure is that, on the whole, actions become more successful as they pass from the sphere of feeling to that of understanding. Our educational belief is that in the long run if men know what they are going to do and how they are going to do it, and what is the nature of the situation with which they are dealing, their response to that situation will be better adjusted and more beneficial than are the responses of the feeling type in like situations.

It is all too obvious that there are limits to the validity of this principle. If men are to investigate, to consider, to decide, then action must be delayed and we must pay the penalty of waiting. If men are to endeavor to understand and know their situations, then we must be prepared to see them make mistakes in their thinking, lose their certainty of touch, wander off into pitfalls and illusions and fallacies of thought, and in consequence secure for the time results far lower in value than those of the instinctive response which they seek to replace. The delays and mistakes and uncertainties of our thinking are a heavy price to pay, but it is the conviction of the teacher that the price is as nothing when compared with the goods which it buys. You may point out to him the loss when old methods of procedure give way before the criticism of understanding, you may remind him of the pain and

suffering when old habits of thought and action
are replaced, you may reprove him for all the
blunders of the past; but in spite of it all he
knows and you know that in human lives taken
separately and in human life as a whole men's
greatest lack is the lack of understanding, their
greatest hope to know themselves and the world
in which they live.

Within the limits of this general educational
principle the place of the liberal college may
easily be fixed. In the technical school pupils
are prepared for a specific work and are kept
for the most part on the plane of perceptual action, doing work which others understand. In
the professional school, students are properly
within the realm of ideas and principles, but they
are still limited to a specific human interest with
which alone their understanding is concerned.
But the college is called liberal as against both
of these because the instruction is dominated by
no special interest, is limited to no single human
tasks, but is intended to take human activity
as a whole, to understand human endeavors
not in their isolation but in their relations to
one another and to the total experience which
we call the life of our people. And just as
we believe that the building of ships has be-

come more successful as men have come to a knowledge of the principles involved in their construction; just as the practice of medicine has become more successful as we have come to a knowledge of the human body, of the conditions within it and the influences without; just so the teacher in the liberal college believes that life as a total enterprise, life as it presents itself to each one of us in his career as an individual—human living—will be more successful in so far as men come to understand it and to know it as they attempt to carry it on.   To give boys an intellectual grasp on human experience—this it seems to me is the teacher's conception of the chief function of the liberal college.

May I call attention to the fact that this second answer of the teacher defines the aim of the college as avowedly and frankly practical. Knowledge is to be sought chiefly for the sake of its contribution to the other activities of human living.   But on the other hand, it is as definitely declared that in method the college is fully and unreservedly intellectual.   If we can see that these two demands are not in conflict but that they stand together in the harmonious relation of means and ends, of instrument and achievement, of method and result, we may escape many a needless conflict and keep our educational policy in singleness of aim and action. To do this we must show that the college is intellectual, not as opposed to practical interests and purposes, but as opposed to unpractical and unwise methods of work. The issue is not between practical and intellectual aims but between the immediate and the remote aim, between the hasty and the measured procedure, between the demand for results at once and the willingness to wait for the best results. The intellectual road to success is longer and more roundabout than any other, but they who are strong and willing for the climbing are brought to higher levels of achievement than they could possibly have attained had they gone straight forward in the pathway of quick returns. If this were not true the liberal college would have no proper place in our life at all. In so far as it is true the college has a right to claim the best of our young men to give them its preparation for the living they are to do.

§ 4

But now that we have attempted to interpret the intellectual mission of the college, it may be fair to ask: ''Are the teachers and scholars of our day always faithful to that mission? Do their statements and their practice always ring in accord with the principle which has been stated?" It seems to me that at two points they are constantly off the key, constantly at variance with the reasons by which alone their teaching can be justified.

In the first place, it often appears as if our teachers and scholars were deliberately in league to mystify and befog the popular mind regarding this practical value of intellectual work. They seem not to wish too much said about the results and benefits. Their desire is to keep aloft the intellectual banner, to proclaim the intellectual gospel, to demand of student and public alike adherence to the faith. And in general when they are questioned as to results they give little satisfaction except to those who are already pledged to unwavering confidence in their *ipse dixit*. And largely as a result of this attitude the American people seem to me to have little understanding of the intellectual work of the college. Our citizens and patrons can see the value of games and physical exercises; they readily perceive the importance of the social give and take of a college democracy; they can appreciate the value of studies which prepare a young man for his profession and so anticipate or replace the professional school; they can even believe that if a boy is kept at some sort of thinking for four years his mind may become more acute, more systematic, more accurate, and hence more useful than it was before. But as for the content of a college course, as for the value of knowledge, what a boy gains by knowing Greek or economics, philosophy or literature, history or biology, except as they are regarded as having professional usefulness, I think our friends are in the dark and are likely to remain so until we turn on the light. When our teachers say, as they sometimes do say, that the effect of knowledge upon the character and life of the student must always be for the college an accident, a circumstance which has no essential connection with its real aim or function, then it seems to me that our educational policy is wholly out of joint. If there be no essential connection between instruction and life, then there is no reason for giving instruction except in so far as it is pleasant in itself, and we have no educational policy at all. As against this hesitancy, this absence of a conviction, we men of the college should declare in clear and unmistakable terms our creed—the creed that knowledge is justified by its results. We should say to our people so plainly that they cannot misunderstand: "Give us your boys, give us the means we need, and we will so train and inform the minds of those boys that their own lives and the lives of the men about them shall be more successful than they could be without our training. Give us our chance and we will show your boys what human living is, for we are convinced that they can live better in knowledge than they can in ignorance."

There is a second wandering from the faith which is so common among investigators that it may fairly be called the "fallacy of the scholar." It is the belief that all knowledge is so good that all parts of knowledge are equally good. Ask many of our scholars and teachers what subjects a boy should study in order that he may gain insight for human living, and they will say, "It makes no difference in what department of knowledge he studies; let him go into Sanskrit or bacteriology, into mathematics or history; if only he goes where men are actually dealing with intellectual problems, and if only he learns how to deal with problems himself, the aim of education is achieved, he has entered into intellectual activity." This point of view, running through all the varieties of the elective system, seems to me hopelessly at variance with any sound educational doctrine. It represents the scholar of the day at his worst both as a thinker and as a teacher. In so far as it dominates a group of college teachers it seems to me to render them unfit to determine and to administer a college curriculum. It is an announcement that they have no guiding principles in their educational practice, no principles of selection in their arrangement of studies, no genuine grasp on the relationship between knowledge and life. It is the concerted statement of a group of men each of whom is lost within the limits of his own special studies, and who as a group seem not to realize the organic relationships between them nor the common task which should bind them together.

In bringing this second criticism against our scholars I am not urging that the principle of election of college studies should be entirely discontinued. But I should like to inquire by what right and within what limits it is justified. The most familiar argument in its favor is that if a student is allowed to choose along the lines of his own intellect or professional interest he will have enthusiasm, the eagerness which comes with the following of one's own bent. Now, just so

far as this result is achieved, just so far as the
quality of scholarship is improved, the procedure
is good and we may follow it if we do not thereby
lose other results more valuable than our gain.
But if the special interest comes into conflict with
more fundamental ones, if what the student pre-
fers is opposed to what he ought to prefer, then
we of the college cannot leave the choice with
him. We must say to him frankly: "If you do
not care for liberal training you had better go
elsewhere; we have a special and definite task
assigned us which demands that we keep free
from the domination of special or professional
pursuits. So long as we are faithful to that task
we cannot give you what you ask."

In my opinion, however, the fundamental motive of the elective system is not the one which
has been mentioned. In the last resort our teachers allow students to choose their own studies
not in order to appeal to intellectual or to professional interest, but because they themselves have
no choice of their own in which they believe with
sufficient intensity to impose it upon their pupils.
And this lack of a dominating educational policy
is in turn an expression of an intellectual attitude, a point of view, which marks the scholars of
our time. In a word, it seems to me that our

willingness to allow students to wander about in the college curriculum is one of the most characteristic expressions of a certain intellectual agnosticism, a kind of intellectual bankruptcy, into which, in spite of all our wealth of information, the spirit of the time has fallen. Let me explain my meaning.

The old classical curriculum was founded by men who had a theory of the world and of human life. They had taken all the available content of human knowledge and had wrought it together into a coherent whole. What they knew was, as judged by our standards, very little in amount. But upon that little content they had expended all the infinite pains of understanding and interpretation. They had taken the separate judgments of science, philosophy, history, and the arts, and had so welded them together, so established their relationships with one another, so freed them from contradictions and ambiguities that, so far as might be in their day and generation, human life as a whole and the world about us were known, were understood, were rationalized. They had a knowledge of human experience by which they could live and which they could teach to others engaged in the activities of living.

But with the invention of methods of scientific investigation and discovery there came pouring into the mind of Europe great masses of intellectual material—astronomy, physics, chemistry. This content for a time it could not understand, could not relate to what it already knew. The old boundary-lines did not inclose the new fields; the old explanations and interpretations would not fit the new facts. Knowledge had not grown, it had simply been enlarged, and the two masses of content, the old and the new, stood facing each other with no common ground of understanding. Here was the intellectual task of the great leaders of the early modern thought of Europe: to re-establish the unity of knowledge, to discover the relationships between these apparently hostile bodies of judgments, to know the world again, but with all the added richness of the new insights and the new information. This was the work of Leibnitz and Spinoza, of Kant and Hegel, and those who labored with them. And in a very considerable measure the task had been accomplished, order had been restored. But again with the inrush of the newer discoveries, first in the field of biology and then later in the world of human relationships, the difficulties have returned, multiplied a thousandfold. Every day sees a new field of facts opened up, a new method of investigation invented, a new department of knowledge established. And in the rush of it all these new sciences come merely as additions, not to be understood but simply numbered, not to be interpreted but simply listed in the great collection of separate fields of knowledge. If you will examine the work of any scientist within one of these fields you will find him ordering, systematizing, reducing to principles, in a word, knowing every fact in terms of its relation to every other fact and to the whole field within which it falls. But at the same time these separate sciences, these separate groups of judgment, are left standing side by side with no intelligible connections, no establishment of relationships, no interpretation in the sense in which we insist upon it within each of the fields taken by itself. Is it not the characteristic statement of a scholar of our time to say: "I do not know what may be the ultimate significance of these facts and these principles; all that I know is that if you will follow my methods within my field you will find the facts coming into order, the principles coming into simple and coherent arrangement. With any problems apart from this order and this arrangement I have intellectually no concern."

It has become an axiom with us that the genuine
student labors within his own field. And if the
student ventures forth to examine the relations
of his field to the surrounding country he very
easily becomes a popularizer, a litterateur, a
speculator, and worst of all, unscientific. Now I
do not object to a man's minding his own intellectual business if he chooses to do so, but when a
man minds his own business because he does not
know any other business, because he has no
knowledge whatever of the relationships which
justify his business and make it worth while,
then I think one may say that though such a man
minds his own affairs he does not know them,
he does not understand them.   Such a man, from
the point of view of the demands of a liberal education, differs in no essential respect from the
tradesman who does not understand his trade or
the professional man who merely practises his
profession. Just as truly as they, he is shut up
within a special interest; just as truly as they he
is making no intellectual attempt to understand
his experience in its unity.   And the pity of it is
that more and more the chairs in our colleges are
occupied by men who have only this special interest, this specialized information, and it is
through them that we attempt to give our boys

a liberal education, which the teachers themselves
have not achieved.

I should not like to be misunderstood in making
this railing accusation against our teachers and
our time. If I say that our knowledge is at present a collection of scattered observations about
the world rather than an understanding of it,
fairness compels the admission that the failure
is due to the inherent difficulties of the situation
and to the novelty of the problems presented. If
I cry out against the agnosticism of our people
it is not as one who has escaped from it, nor as
one who would point the way back to the older
synthesis, but simply as one who believes that the
time has come for a reconstruction, for a new
synthesis. We have had time enough now to get
some notion of our bearings, shocks enough to
get over our nervousness and discomfiture when
a new one comes along. It is the opportunity and
the obligation of this generation to think through
the content of our knowing once again, to understand it, so far as we can. And in such a battle
as this, surely it is the part of the college to take
the lead. Here is the mission of the college
teacher as of no other member of our common
life. Surely he should stand before his pupils
and before all of us as a man who has achieved

some understanding of this human situation of
ours, but more than that, as one who is eager
for the conflict with the powers of darkness and
who can lead his pupils in enthusiastic devotion
to the common cause of enlightenment.

§ 5

And now, finally, after these attacks upon the
policies which other men have derived from their
love of knowledge, may I suggest two matters of
policy which seem to me to follow from the definition of education which we have taken. The
first concerns the content of the college course;
the second has to do with the method of its
presentation to the undergraduate.

We have said that the system of free election
is natural for those to whom knowledge is simply
a number of separate departments. It is equally
true that just in so far as knowledge attains
unity, just so far as the relations of the various
departments are perceived, freedom of election
by the student must be limited. For it at once
appears that on the one side there are vast ranges
of information which have virtually no significance for the purposes of a liberal education,
while on the other hand there are certain ele-

ments so fundamental and vital that without any one of them a liberal education is impossible.

I should like to indicate certain parts of human knowledge which seem to me so essential that no principle of election should ever be allowed to drive them out of the course of any college student.

First, a student should become acquainted with the fundamental motives and purposes and beliefs which, clearly or unclearly recognized, underlie all human experience and bind it together. He must perceive the moral strivings, the intellectual endeavors, the esthetic experiences of his race, and closely linked with these, determining and determined by them, the beliefs about the world which have appeared in our systems of religion. To investigate this field, to bring it to such clearness of formulation as may be possible, is the task of philosophy—an essential element in any liberal education. Secondly, as in human living, our motives, purposes and beliefs have found expression in institutions—those concerted modes of procedure by which we work together—a student should be made acquainted with these. He should see and appreciate what is intended, what accomplished, and what left undone by such institutions as property, the courts, the family, the church, the mill. To know these as contributing and failing to contribute to human welfare is the work of our social or humanistic sciences, into which a boy must go on his way through the liberal college. Thirdly, in order to understand the motives and the institutions of human life one must know the conditions which surround it, the stage on which the game is played. To give this information is the business of astronomy, geology, physics, chemistry, biology and the other descriptive sciences. These a boy must know, so far as they are significant and relevant to his purpose. Fourthly, as all three of these factors, the motives, the institutions, the natural processes have sprung from the past and have come to be what they are by change upon change in the process of time, the student of human life must try to learn the sequence of events from which the present has come. The development of human thought and attitude, the development of human institutions, the development of the world and of the beings about us—all these must be known, as throwing light upon present problems, present instrumentalities, present opportunities in the life of human endeavor. And in addition to these four studies which render human experience in terms of abstract ideas, a liberal education must take account of those concrete representations of life which are given in the arts, and especially in the art of literature. It is well that a boy should be acquainted with his world not simply as expressed by the principles of knowledge but also as depicted by the artist with all the vividness and definiteness which are possible in the portrayal of individual beings in individual relationships. These five elements, then, a young man must take from a college of liberal training, the contributions of philosophy, of humanistic science, of natural science, of history, and of literature. So far as knowledge is concerned, these at least he should have, welded together in some kind of interpretation of his own experience and of the world in which he lives.

My second suggestion is that our college curriculum should be so arranged and our instruction so devised that its vital connection with the living of men should be obvious even to an undergraduate. A little while ago I heard one of the most prominent citizens of this country speaking of his college days, and he said, "I remember so vividly those few occasions on which the professor would put aside the books and talk like a real man about real things." Oh, the bitterness

of those words to the teacher! Our books are
not dealing with the real things, and for the most
part we are not real men either, but just old
fogies and bookworms. And to be perfectly
frank about the whole matter, I believe that in
large measure our pupils are indifferent to their
studies simply because they do not see that these
are important.

Now if we really have a vital course of study
to present I believe that this difficulty can in large
measure be overcome. It is possible to make a
freshman realize the need of translating his experience from the forms of feeling to those of
ideas. He can and he ought to be shown that
now, his days of mere tutelage being over, it is
time for him to face the problems of his people,
to begin to think about those problems for himself, to learn what other men have learned and
thought before him, in a word, to get himself
ready to take his place among those who are
responsible for the guidance of our common life
by ideas and principles and purposes. If this
could be done, I think we should get from the
reality-loving American boy something like an
intellectual enthusiasm, something of the spirit
that comes when he plays a game that seems to
him really worth playing. But I do not believe

that this result can be achieved without a radical reversal of the arrangement of the college curriculum. I should like to see every freshman at once plunged into the problems of philosophy, into the difficulties and perplexities about our institutions, into the scientific accounts of the world especially as they bear on human life, into the portrayals of human experience which are given by the masters of literature. If this were done by proper teaching, it seems to me the boy's college course would at once take on significance for him; he would understand what he is about; and though he would be a sadly puzzled boy at the end of the first year, he would still have before him three good years of study, of investigation, of reflection, and of discipleship, in which to achieve, so far as may be, the task to which he has been set. Let him once feel the problems of the present, and his historical studies will become significant; let him know what other men have discovered and thought about his problems, and he will be ready to deal with them himself. But in any case, the whole college course will be unified and dominated by a single interest, a single purpose—that of so understanding human life as to be ready and equipped for the practice of it. And this would mean for the college, not another seeking of the way of quick returns, but rather an escape from aimless wanderings in the mere by-paths of knowledge, a resolute climbing on the highroad to a unified grasp upon human experience.

I have taken so much of your time this morning that an apology seems due for the things I have omitted to mention. I have said nothing of the organization of the college, nothing of the social life of the students, nothing of the relations with the alumni, nothing of the needs and qualifications of the teachers, and, even within the consideration of the course of study, nothing of the value of specialization or of the disciplinary subjects or of the training of language and expression. And I have put these aside deliberately, for the sake of a cause which is greater than any of them—a cause which lies at the very heart of the liberal college. It is the cause of making clear to the American people the mission of the teacher, of convincing them of the value of knowledge: not the specialized knowledge which contributes to immediate practical aims, but the unified understanding which is Insight.

THE UNITY OF THE CURRICULUM

"The New Republic," October 25, 1922

THE UNITY OF THE CURRICULUM

ONE cannot talk about the unity of the curriculum without talking about the unity of knowledge. And one hesitates to talk about the unity of knowledge because one does not know what to say. It is just this "hesitation" which is the most striking feature of current educational policy. How to escape from it is a very pressing and a very difficult problem.

We commonly say of the elective system that it has cut the course of study into a multitude of disconnected parts. It has also allowed the pupil to make an education by taking a very few out of the great number of these separate items. Under this system then the question is, "How shall we make out a few disconnected fragments of knowledge a unified understanding of knowledge as a whole, as a single thing?"

To this question there are two familiar answers. The first is that the question itself is nonsense. According to this view knowledge as a whole has no unity. Knowing is a number of relatively separate investigations. No one man can be acquainted with all these lines of inquiry. And if he were, he could not make them into a single meaning, a unitary scheme of understanding. In a word, the unity of knowledge is a myth.

For the men who take this point of view, the theory of the curriculum is a very simple thing. For them the chief end and aim of instruction is command of a "subject." They see, of course, that no subject can be studied in complete isolation. Every subject is surrounded and affected by two sets of relations of which its students must take account. First, it must be known in relation to other subjects in the same "group." One cannot know economics well without understanding history, politics, and law; to get hold of biology one must learn chemistry and psychology, too; subjects in the same group do run into each other. And, second, subjects must be studied in relation to their practical applications. After all, it is forever and necessarily true that the function of knowledge is to illumine and direct practical activity. One does not, then, know his subject unless he sees it as an instrument of control in the practical situations with which it is intended to deal.

In the light of these two excellent and modifying principles, the disbelievers in the unity of knowledge proceed to their teaching task. They select some interest, some fragment of knowledge which seen in its immediate relations is not too big to be grasped by a single mind. This is their major subject; to it they give their major attention. Commonly, however, they insist upon minor interests as well. In order to be a well rounded man one should take pieces of work in other fields. [There should be given to every student a little music, a taste of philosophy, a glimpse into history, some practice in the technique of the laboratory, a thrill or two in the appreciation of poetry. These specifics will secure one's general mental health against the dangers of one-sidedness.] Through it all there runs the quality of the devil at church on Sunday resting from the labors of a busy week. We do well to remember that in this point of view there is no pervading unity.

With respect to the origin and influence of the view just stated, two statements may be made. They are very complimentary to natural science, but are easily interpreted as attacks upon it. First, it is chiefly natural science which is responsible for the opinion that knowledge has no unity. Second, it is chiefly that view which has brought our college teaching into incoherence and confusion. In my opinion it seems probable that the most important fact connected with the development of the elective system in America is that Charles William Eliot was a chemist. So far as I know he is the greatest leader in collegiate policy that America has had. But the modes of thought of his powerful leadership were predominantly the mechanical forms of chemical analysis. Those forms, with all their values and all their limitations, he for a long time fixed upon the academic thinking of this country.

I have intimated that the double statement just made is not intended as hostile to science, nor as casting aspersions upon the native intelligence of the scientist, or the necessity of his work. What it does mean to say is that the natural sciences deal with a type of content which invites and makes possible the isolation of problems to a degree not achieved in other types of investigation. If he have proper regard for related subjects, the scientific student can define his task as a separate and distinct piece of work, can adjust his technique to the dealing with it, and can then go serenely about his labor knowing that it, by itself, will lead him as far and farther than he

can ever attain. Wars may come and go, king-
doms rise and fall, schools of poetry flourish and
decay, fashions bloom and fade, and through
them all the egg-secretions stand secure. "What
have they been? What have they done? What
are they made of? What will they do?" If once
he be wedded to questions like these, surely a man
may settle down and live in bliss forever after.
But can he? What of the state of learning within
which the happy union is carried on? Has any
state been able yet to live in anarchy? One
wishes that it might be done, that every man
might go his way, follow his bent and find himself
at peace with every other man. But that is not
the actual situation in the world with which we
deal. Out of the purposes and acts of many men,
society must make a plan, a scheme of common
living. Out of the thoughts of many men, our
scholarship must make a plan, such common
dominating scheme as can be made. But just at
present, common schemes of thought have broken
down. The sciences are not explained, not understood. Rightly enough, they will not knuckle under to schemes of thought devised before their
principles were known. Thought must be made
anew to take them in and give them proper place.
But when they stand upon the ruins of an older

scheme which they have smashed, and cry, "Down with the state, we 'll have no state at all!" they talk familiar nonsense. Because another scheme of thought has broken down, they think that schemes of thought are gone forever, that unity in knowledge is a myth. What science tells them that? Have they not gone outside their premises? They were to live and work each with his problem, by himself. But when they say that strings of separate thoughts are what the common thought should be, they have a plan for common thought. And they have made it badly because their thinking, their technique, was made for other problems. To make of science a philosophy is just as bad as finding scientific fact in myth and fable. Let each man do his task. But let us not infer that since one man cannot do another's work, the second, too, is likewise helpless in the field for which he is equipped.

But now already while discussing the first answer to our leading question, we have arrived at the second. If it is not nonsense to seek for unity in knowledge, then it is nonsense not to seek it. And in fact this seeking is the great intellectual undertaking of this time and of a renewing civilization. Just as each science within its field brings facts to unity, attempts to understand

them, just so these separate sciences are facts
which we must unify if we would understand
them all. To understand them is to know them
as a single meaning with separate parts. In this
sense, knowing is always unifying. And when
one makes this statement one does not say the
work is done: one does not offer a reconstructed
world already made. One says that here we have
a task which faces learning at the present time.
Upon this task our scholarship must work, not
saying in advance what will be found, but trying
to find the forms of unity which must be there if
we can think at all. And teaching, liberal teaching, is just the attempt to put our students at
work upon that task. They have a world to find,
to make. It is our task to set them at it.

I think that perhaps the best way of explaining this second answer to our question will be
to apply it to one or two specific proposals which
are at present under consideration. What is the
value of preliminary survey courses in giving
unity to study? My impression is that the value
is real but rather slight. In general the plan
is that as he approaches a group of subjects, a
student shall be given an outline account of these,
their problems, their procedures, their relations
to one another. This is a device of which the

social sciences are fond. I have heard the teachers of these sciences discuss with much eagerness the question, "How can the social sciences be unified?" May I record the opinion that in themselves these studies have no dominating unity? To tell of their relations to one another is not to unify them, unless it means to tell their common dependence upon other studies outside the list. Logic and ethics have, I think, the principles of unity for all our social studies. And if we seek for unity without them, we get a list of separate things quite shorn of all the deeper meanings which they ought to have. And so against the survey course which lists, describes, and classifies a group of studies, I would suggest the analytic course which finds a method of thought and gives a student practice in it. To get a student ready for a group of studies, one should select a problem which demands the proper kind of thinking, a certain way of gathering information, a way of asking questions, a way of answering them, and then should set the student's mind at work in just those ways. I would not make the opposition here too sharp. One must have proper content if one would practise proper method. And yet it is true that survey as such, the listing of problems and answers

in fields which one has never seen—this in itself
is not sufficient introduction. If one can get the
student thinking in a given way and set him loose
amid the content, that way will lead him to the
problems and their differences. An introductory
course should lead a student not so much by content as by method, not so much by answer as by
problem, not only by external list of separate
studies, but also by the dialectic of a mode of
thought which seeks and finds the content which
it feeds upon.

And again, if we are to count upon a single
course to unify the college studies, should freshmen or seniors take the course? At present, I
think two courses are needed, one for beginners
in the college work and one to bring the studies all
together at the end. But as between the two, if
we must choose, the latter would seem to be the
more important. I think that every liberal college should demand of all its students that they
attempt to relate their various studies into some
ordered scheme of thought. Within the various
subjects they have taken they should begin to
see the principles of thinking, the system of
values, the fundamental notions which underlie
and dominate all that we think and do. I know
that I am saying here that in its essence a liberal

course of study must be a study in philosophy.
But one must say just that because it is the truth.
And we who send our students out with scattered
studies never brought together, without a notion
of the mode of thought by which the fundamental
unifying motives may be found, are not giving
liberal education. Our seniors must be made to
attempt the task of having a philosophy.

And here at last we come, I think, to the only
important thing that can be said about the unity
of the curriculum and our relation to it. The
essential fact is that we, the college teachers, have
no philosophy. We have been trained within the
elective system. We are the devotees of ''subjects.'' We live and think amid the fragments of
an intellectual world which has been broken
down. Ours is the task of building up again another view of life to hold the meanings which we
had and have. And if we shirk that task in study
and in teaching, no unifying courses will repair
the damage. If teachers think in fragments, they
cannot teach in wholes. Devices of teaching
technique will never remedy defects of thought.
All that a teacher has to give is just his way of
thinking about the world. And if we mean to
give a liberal education, then we must be ourselves a group of liberally educated men. Out of

the turmoil and confusion of this present time our minds must seek, are seeking order and meaning. And as we find it our students will find it, too. We do not teach so much by what we say as by the way we think. Our liberal colleges, teachers and students alike, have the task of finding and using a mode of thought by which an understanding of our life in all its phases may some day be achieved. Our urgent problem, whether in teaching or in study, is not to find devices which may remedy defects inherent in our usual way of doing things. The problem is so to construe our task that we shall be about it in methods suited to it. We must not hesitate, dallying with "subjects," when the unity of knowing is before us as our goal. The time has come for vigorous and decisive action. It is a time of genuine testing of the American college and of its teachers.

REORGANIZING THE CURRICULUM

A PART OF THE PRESIDENT'S REPORT, 1918

REORGANIZING THE CURRICULUM[1]

THE longer one attempts to devise a liberal training by the additions and combinations of courses, the more one becomes convinced that addition is an illusion and that courses are the chimeras of an imagination perverted by the categories of mechanics. ⌐Twenty courses do not make a college education any more than twenty legs make a man, nor twenty heads, nor even ten hearts, two legs, and eight fingers⌐ And in the same way three courses do not make an intellectual interest, an experience of the actual process of the working mind. Something is wrong with the terms, something is radically wrong with the process of combining them.

What is the trouble? It seems to me very clear that the concepts of quantity and measurement have wrecked the organic unity of the college course. In making elective courses we have felt the genuine need of uniformity and so have established units in terms of which to measure. And having established our separate units of subjects,

---

[1] This report has already appeared in "The Liberal College" with the title of "A Reorganization of the College Curriculum."

courses, departments, we have felt free to pluck them out of the living organism one by one, to substitute one for another, and then to put them back supposing the life process to be still rushing on in spite of all our interruptions.

If this be true, then no re-sorting of the courses will gain the ends we seek. Rather, it seems to me, we must re-think our terms and reconsider our procedure. I am inclined, therefore, to recommend to the trustees and faculty of the college a fairly fundamental transformation of its organization. You will not find in this suggestion the slightest hint of any change of purpose. You will, however, find a strong conviction that the college organization in which that purpose finds expression is quite inadequate. I am proposing, therefore, that a new one take its place.

As we have postulated two aims in the defining of a liberal education, so I would, in good mechanical form, propose the division of the college into two separate colleges, a Junior and a Senior College. And if it be at once retorted that this is a vicious mechanical separation in purpose and in method, then I would reply that the division into two, if discreetly made, is not so bad as a division into twenty, and further that, in spite of bad appearances, this division of ours is not to be me-

chanical—never shall we take these colleges apart
or try to substitute them for one another in any
known relationship.

But now to state our plan in sober, honest
terms! Our purpose is, we say, to set men on the
road toward liberal education. And liberal education seems to have two aspects: (1) that of general apprehension of the culture of one's race and
(2) that of feeling of the actual process of the
mind by which that culture has been made and
still is in the making. These aims are always
present wherever a liberal college is. But they
are often obscure in content and so hazy in outline
as to be mistaken one for the other. ⌞Men say
"any course of study properly pursued is liberal"
and so they take some ten or twenty courses, each
of necessity improperly pursued and call the process liberal. Men say "a little of everything and
everything of something—that gives a liberal education." But they forget that knowledge when
made up of "everythings" and "somethings" is
not real knowledge at all—not knowledge in the
sense of wisdom or of understanding, nor
even knowledge in the actual process of its
making.⌟

It seems to me essential that these two aims
should be kept clear and kept apart for fear that

either may be lost or either substituted for the other. I would propose, therefore, that we establish them and build them into the very structure of the college course. [Let us have two colleges instead of one, or better two in one, the first explicitly devoted to the general aim, the second, in greater part at least, given up to special studies, and both together mastered by the common aim of trying to understand and share the labor and ecstasy of human knowledge and human apprehension.]

How shall it be done? In its most external aspect the college is, of course, an institution which, having instructed students, or perhaps not having instructed them, examines them in order to determine whether or not to give them a degree which certifies that they are, in some sense agreed upon, educated men. In this external sense, one college is one set of examinations with all that thereunto belongs. If then we should establish two examinations, two sets of tests, we should in this external sense divide the four-year college into two parts, each of two years. From this would follow various results as to our methods of teaching, methods of study, methods of life. According as men are to be examined so will their modes of living be. Two aims, two sets of examinations; hence two colleges—that is the program.

I would propose then that at the end of the sophomore year we establish a set of tests or one comprehensive test to determine whether or not in their two years of college work our students have been making headway toward intelligence, toward culture, toward an apprehension of human knowledge as a whole. And at the end of the senior year we should have a second test which, taking the first for granted, should try to discover what students know of some one field of knowledge, what work is done within it and what it means. Passing the first examination would give admission to the Senior College. Passing the senior test would qualify a student for his degree.

It would be essential, I think, that such examinations be set, not by the teachers who have given the instruction but by an examining board appointed for the purpose. Teachers would still continue to give their tests at the endings of courses, and passing one's courses might be made a prerequisite for admission to the general examination. And the board of examiners might perhaps include some of the teachers of the college whose work is being examined. But in principle, it seems to me, courses and examinations should be kept far apart. The board should set its tests not on the basis of courses taken but by the guidance of an end to be achieved, a type of education to be realized. We should examine the student, not his knowledge of the courses he has taken.

I should like now to suggest some of the advantages which it seems to me such an arrangement would bring about in the two colleges which are established by it.

Junior College. The first advantage of the arrangement in the Junior College would be the clarifying and validating of what the college community means by culture. It would give to the younger members of the community a compelling sense of something that must be done, some quality that must be taken on, some power that must be gained, some sensitiveness that must be won. There is now no such compelling sense of common purpose and requirement in our conglomerate arrangement of courses. In a recent pronunciamento of the largest association of colleges in the United States, it was argued that since the concept of liberal education has no generally accepted meaning, a given subject might just as well be included in the college course as any other; apparently no one could tell the difference in the result. And if our college authorities are in a haze like this, there is no wonder that freshmen and sophomores feel no compulsion of a clear and definite purpose driving them on. But we must have just that to make our college work worth while—a recognition by us all that there are certain things which one must know, must feel, must see, must understand if he desires to be regarded as a member of this community. Unless he does the things we do and loves the things we love, he is not one of us. I think perhaps we might regard the Junior College examinations as a matriculation test, the college having given a man two years in which to show that he may rightly claim a place as one who is her own.

And may I hasten to say that the merit of such an examination as this would not lie in a great severity. I see no reason why it should be in general quality harder than any of the tests we give at present. The elimination of many students by rigid tests might easily be done. But I am not convinced that education by such elimination is the thing most needed in the American colleges just now. There would be much to be gained in private satisfaction and in high quality of scholarly achievement by the elimination of all students except the very best. But that is not the gain most sorely needed at the present time. Our task, the most important task, is that of taking the average American boy and those above the average and trying to make of them men of cultured power. No one doubts that this work can be done for boys of unusual gifts and aptitude. But what can be done in general? What are the possibilities of cultural education in the country at large? That seems to me the urgent, the almost terrifying question which now confronts our colleges of liberal education. May I say again, therefore, that the merit of this examination would be, not in this or that established degree of severity, but in the setting of a standard as such, in the making clear that "liberal" has a meaning which cuts like steel between the groups of those who are and those who are not liberal sophomores.

At this point there is a question which I know is quite inevitable: "Upon what subjects will you examine at the end of the sophomore year? The student has passed his courses one by one and answered questions on them. Will you ask further questions on these courses? Will your examination mean a grand and general review?"

May I try to answer the question in two parts, distinguishing between the method and the content of the mind with which the examination is to deal?

If we were examining the intellectual method of a sophomore to see what sort of man he is there are, I think, seven main questions which we should like to ask:

1 Can he and does he read books?

      In books is gathered up the culture and knowledge of the race. A boy who has not learned to go to them, to live in them, to understand their meanings, is not, in method at least, upon the great highroad of education.

2 Can he express his own thoughts in writing?

3 Can he speak clearly and accurately?

4 Can he listen to and understand another's speech?

5 Has he a sense of fact, distinguishing from facts the mere suggestions which are not yet established?

6 Can he derive an implication, draw an inference, and see what implications and inferences do not follow?

7 Has he a sense of values by which to feel,

to appreciate, to recognize the things
worth while from those not worthy of our
choosing?

These are, so far as method is concerned, the
questions I should like to ask about a sophomore
seeking admission to a Senior College. They indicate the qualities of mind which make for education. If one has gained these qualities I think
we might admit him to special studies of a liberal sort. If not, it is a sin to let him think, however many courses he has passed, that he is on
the road to liberal education.

And on the side of content we should again try
to discover not so much what he has done to
courses as what courses, and growing, and being himself, have done to him, what sort of man
he is becoming. He should be examined upon
his knowledge of literature, of natural and humanistic science, should be expected to know the
essential things in them which are the common
stock of men who are trying to interpret the
world in which they live. And further, he should
appreciate and understand in some degree the
purposes and attitudes of men of letters, of
scientists, and other thinkers, should know what
tasks they undertake, what methods they adopt,
what results they have achieved, and what, in

general outline, they now propose to do. Such
an examination would require knowledge of the
subjects taught and studied in the courses, but
it would imply as well a student's independent
reading and thinking about his subjects. It
would, I think, relegate the courses to their
proper place as moments in a process of acquisi-
tion and understanding, a process which every
student must be carrying on himself, a process
which the entire community accepts as that by
which it seeks its purpose of liberal education.

Such an examination could not be given by one
man nor in one day. It would require a board
of examiners and would inevitably extend over
two, three, or four weeks. It would include written examinations, tests, reports, conferences. It
would put into explicit and regular form such
queries and associations as one would wish
to have with a young man whose intellectual
and personal quality one might wish to determine.

But now to return to the listing of the advantages of the Junior College examination! We
have said that over against the separate courses
it would set up the demand of the college as a
whole for rightness of method and rightness of
content in the teaching and study. There are

some other advantages perhaps not so important.

I think the improvement which would be brought to sophomore study would be very great. The sophomore is our least responsible student. The enthusiasm and the docility, perhaps, of the freshman year have somewhat lessened. The ending of the college course is still three years away. The goal toward which it leads is far and indistinct. The sophomore is not under pressure. Such a test as we have outlined, expressing a demand that must be met at the ending of the year, summing up the activities of the two years in one compelling purpose and interest— such a test would in my opinion transform the sophomore year. If so, it would give gain where now our loss is greatest. For many students it would prevent the breaking down of the college course.

Another gain would be, I think, that of placing upon the student the responsibility for the getting of his own education. The college would give no guarantee that courses would cover all the content of the general examination. In the last resort, a student should find out for himself what demand the community lays upon him; he should see that the doing of daily tasks assigned with daily regularity is good but childish. He should undertake to make himself what the college approves, should use his courses and his own self-directed studies as instruments for getting ready for the tests which the college is to give him. In the years from eighteen to twenty-three one should be getting something of the self-reliance of a man. Our present procedure tends too much to keep the students young in will as well as in intelligence.

Still another gain would come in the relations of teachers and students. The present process tends toward being one of handing out and then demanding that the thing received be given back again. The teacher is at the same time examiner. But if teacher and pupil were alike preparing for a distant test which neither is to set, there would be more of comradeship, of teaching and discipleship than we have now.

I hesitate to speak of gains so far as teaching is concerned for, out of my own experience if in no other way, I know how jealous teachers are of their independence, how much they cherish their sovereign right to teach as they think best. And in a certain field of their relations I would not yield to any one in fighting for the teacher's independence. But independence at this other point of which we speak is nothing else than anarchy. May I then suggest two gains that might be won for teaching.

First, I think that the separate courses taken by any student for a common test would find proper relation to each other just through their common relation to the common test. Each course would find itself called upon to play its proper part, each teacher would need to know what other teachers were doing, each would assume the work of other teachers as joining with his own. At present one teacher knows another's work by gossip, often by idle, inaccurate gossip of undergraduates, hardly ever, if at all, by genuine conference. A demand of unified knowledge accepted as the standard of the Junior College, enforced by an examination for membership in the community, would bring about, I think, some understanding of the common task and hence relating of the various ·parts within the unity to which they all belong.

Another gain for teachers would be that in some measure their teaching would be tested. On the whole it is not good for any man to keep on doing work on which no adequate judgment of approval or disapproval is ever passed by competent authority. The tests implied in student popularity, in the number of student elec-

tions in one's courses, in the promotions or re-
fusals of promotion decreed by trustees and
presidents, these do not satisfy our college teachers. They have many, many better reasons for
disgruntlement. But one important cause of dis-
content lies, I think, just in the lack of any sense
of right appraisal of their work. The men who
publish find their judgment among their fellow-
scholars who do not hesitate to speak their minds.
But men who teach mark their own teaching. It
takes a fair amount of self-esteem to keep one's
courage up. And so I think that an objective
test would give relief and on the whole much
satisfaction.

I am sure that there would be great gain in
the separating of freshmen, sophomores, juniors,
and seniors into distinct groups in the arrangement of their courses. If only sophomores were
taking the courses of the second year, and if all
sophomores had taken the same or equivalent
courses in the previous year, both teacher and
pupil would profit by the uniformity. The
course could then be made to lead from something
in the past to something in the future. It would
not be a mere detached unmeaning fragment be-
ginning from so many different sources that it
has no common source at all, and leading into so

many different directions that the word "direction" loses its meaning. The course would tend to be part of a scheme of training, a common training for a group of men seeking the same end, and hence following the same road and traveling together.

There would be, I think, distinct gain in administration, in the simplification of arrangements of hours, schedules, and other like matters. The separation of freshmen and sophomores from upper-classmen in class enrolments would give a genuine gain. If, as would be practically certain, freshmen and sophomores were separated from each other in the arranging of classes, our present difficulties as to schedules would disappear. Perhaps in this way the amount of administration in the colleges might be reduced. I am sure that very much of the time of administrative officers is spent in reconciling the conflicting desires of anxious teachers. Strangely enough, it usually seems that they, the administrative officers, have the desires from which official denials spring. But in any case, probably to the gratification both of teachers and officers, we might in this way diminish administration.

For teachers and students, then, it seems to

me, the proposal of a Junior College is worth considering. It would pledge the community to an end and to a standard. If successful, it would make the concept of a general liberal education a definite one. That concept is compelling enough if only it is perceived and understood. If then, as I think it would, this proposed arrangement should bring our common purpose into clarity and definiteness, it would set us on the road we seek, and I am inclined to think that we should travel it in gay and serious fellowship.

The Senior College. The determining motive of the Senior College would be the second of our aims, to bring a student into actual contact with the working minds by which the knowledge and apprehension of mankind are made. This opportunity would be open to men coming successfully from the Junior College. Here they would find a greater freedom, greater responsibility, and more urgent obligations. My impression is that corresponding to the improvement of attitude in the sophomore year would come a definite gain for juniors and seniors, first from the sense of freedom and personal initiative and second from the compulsion of the higher intellectual comradeship into which they are received.

In the Senior College a very considerable part

of the student's time would be given to one major interest. What does this mean? It does not mean that the work would be confined within what we now call a department. It does mean a group of related studies, taken from several departments, but all bound together by some common interest and so fusing together in terms of some central inquiry or investigation. The nature of this would of course vary with the field.

It does not mean that the student is to enter a professional school at the end of his sophomore year. The college has given very few professional courses in the past, and my impression is that it will give fewer rather than more of them in the future. I am not saying that a student's choice of his major might not be influenced by the profession which he has in view. Probably in many cases this would happen. But I do mean that during the college years the organization of the courses will be in terms of intellectual interests and problems, not in terms of immediate practical pursuits for which specific preparation is needed. Here, of course, is one of the great educational issues of our time which I must not stop to consider at present. May I say simply that the policy of the college thus far seems clear and definite upon the issue; we are a non-professional college—but very practical.

But now positively, what does it mean? I am not willing to dogmatize with great specification until we have had further opportunity to examine the procedure of colleges in which like experiments have been made. I am sure, however, of several points. First, the major should be a course of study arranged under the direction of one teacher or a small group of teachers in related fields. Second, it should be regarded, not as a group of lectures or courses to be taken, but as a study or reading or investigation carried on by the student, to which the lectures of teachers contribute so far as may be. Third, it should have such unity as to admit of a single test upon it all at the close of the course. Fourth, it should be pursued more informally than our present courses, but under the immediate direction of some teacher, acting individually or as representative of a group. Fifth, it should culminate in some report, some thesis, or record of investigation, or in an examination which should give final evidence of the student's ability and achievement. Sixth, the doing of satisfactory work in such a major field should be required for a degree.

There are two beliefs involved in this proposal.

First, juniors and seniors in college are or can be made mature enough in mind and purpose to take on genuine intellectual responsibilities; it is a sin to keep them children. Second, such intellectual responsibility calls for a different, a more informal relationship between teacher and pupil than is desirable in the earlier years.

Such a majoring plan would again postulate a scheme of independent examination for the testing of results. There would not be, of course, such general examining as that upon the work of the Junior College. But there ought to be in each field the submitting of the evidence of the student's work to some independent and recognized authority in that field for judgment of its worth. The student should be informed and record made that he has or has not done something which men of his years and opportunities may reasonably be expected to do.

It is hardly necessary, I think, to speak of the advantages of such an arrangement. The values to students and teachers alike are clearly obvious. For students, the greater freedom, the close association with a small group of men of like interest, the immediate acquaintance with and direction by a small number of teachers, the demand upon one's powers which comes from the acceptance of a definite task, all these would stimulate as well as enlighten the student mind. For the teachers, the reduction of the amount of formal instruction would be a gain. There would be danger that much time would be taken in informal instruction, but this would be so much more near to the teacher's own study that it might in many cases be of help rather than a hindrance to scholarly pursuits. Certainly there would be more of genuine satisfaction in it.

The real question as to such a plan is not, Is it desirable? but, Can it be made to work? And the question is not one to be evaded. But my own conviction is very strong that the thing can be done. I am certain that it ought to be tried. It is better to see what can be accomplished along such a line than to wait ignobly for some one else to make the attempt. As Socrates, in Plato's Euthydemus, when told that in the process of becoming wise a man must lose his ignorant life, offers himself for sacrifice, so may the college do. A death like that would be a noble ending, the sort of ending from which many splendid enterprises have sprung.

I have spoken of the "major" interest in the Senior College. It seems clear that this interest should not claim all of a student's working time.   Until our plans for majors are made more definite, one cannot tell just what the minor arrangement should be.   I would suggest, however, that three fourths of the time be given to the major and one fourth reserved for the minor interests.   In this case it would be necessary to provide in the Senior College courses for men not majoring in the fields in which they lie.   It would be essential also to provide that the minors be taken outside the major fields.   I should not now be willing to go so far as in the report of 1914, requiring all students to take, in junior year, the history of thought and American history, and in the senior year, intellectual and moral problems.   But it would seem to me essential that the general interest which controls the Junior College should not be wholly put aside.   At least we should maintain a balancing of interest by requiring study outside the major field.   It would not do to let our special study drive away the fundamental aim which we would make it serve, the aim of so knowing and feeling our human life and men's interpretations of it that one is free in living it.   We must remain in general apprehension as well as in special study a liberal college.

Conclusion.   There are many details to be

worked out before such a reorganization as I have proposed could be adopted. The most fundamental and the most difficult is that of the establishing of examining boards wholly or in part distinct from the teaching faculty. This separation of the two functions of teaching and examining is not in one sense essential to the plan. Clearly the Junior and Senior Colleges could be set apart each with its own peculiar work, each with its own preliminary and final examinations —this could be done without so sharp a separation between teaching and examining. And yet the separation is suggested by the plan and would in my opinion contribute largely to its success. How far are we willing to go along this line? Are we ready to establish two boards of examiners correlative with the teaching faculty? If so, shall the faculty participate in the appointment of such boards, or shall it be wholly in the hands of the trustees and president? This is a set of issues difficult to deal with. They are to be met for the sake of the realizing of the purpose of the college.

As I close this discussion, I can merely call attention to important questions which are bound up with the project which we have been considering.

The required studies of the Junior College would presumedly not differ radically from the present requirements of the first and second years. I think that we are approaching settlement of the questions regarding the studies of these years.

The reorganization proposed would have great effect upon our dealings with the members of the faculty, those now with us as well as others to be appointed. For the trying of a high experiment we must have men of high ability and courage. It is the primary task of the college to make its provision for teachers conformable to the demands upon them.

There is no implication in the plan of any radical change in our methods of admitting students. Such changes might be suggested by later experience, but they are not apparent now.

Before such a plan could be put into operation it would be essential that we make careful study of like attempts in other institutions and in other countries. The most radical change in the conduct of the teaching is in the system of majoring in the Senior College. Here we must go carefully but with not too much delay.

To sum it all up, may I say that the cause of liberal education is crying aloud for intelligent and resolute support. It will not do just now to stand on the defensive. Liberal teaching must be established. If this is to be done we must go on; we are just emerging from a period of vast confusion and distraction in educational theory and practice. It is a time for knowing what you propose to do and how it is to be done—and for doing it.